MATCHED

Insider tips & tricks from a
former Pharmacy Residency
Program Director

BRIAN LEONARD, PHARMD

Copyright © 2020 by Brian Leonard, PharmD.

All rights reserved. This book is protected by copyright. No part of this book may be reproduced or transmitted in any form or by any means, including as photocopies or scanned-in or other electronic copies, or utilized by any information storage and retrieval system without written permission from the copyright owner.

ISBN: 9798554467394

Printed in the United States of America.

Cover Design by 100Covers.com
Interior Design by FormattedBooks.com

DESCRIPTION

To date, 2020 saw the lowest pharmacy residency match rate and highest number of unmatched candidates. As the job market continues to shrink and advanced training becomes the minimum standard for even entry-level positions, the importance of securing a residency has become paramount. After serving as a residency preceptor, program coordinator, and program director, I have repeatedly encountered too many underprepared and overwhelmed applicants. Formal education and training focus on pharmacology, pharmacotherapy, and practical applications, yet the necessary skills of effective self-promotion and interviewing are often neglected. My goal is to help you learn everything you need to help you prepare and ease the stress of the residency matching process: objective self-evaluation, effective application materials, the art of interviewing, example interview questions and answers, and more (with infamous *AnecDose* examples along the way). Let me be your personal guide as I reveal insider tips and tricks to help you understand the mind of residency program directors and get MATCHED.

DEDICATION

To Karen and Karen, without whom I would have never gotten into ambulatory care or become a residency program director.

And to my wife, the best thing I got out of pharmacy school.

INTRODUCTION

Congratulations on choosing to dedicate yourself to the practice of pharmacy and striving for advanced clinical training through completion of a residency program. As a former residency program director, my goals for you are twofold: 1) to submit effective and memorable application materials to receive as many interview invitations as possible and 2) to successfully navigate the interview gauntlet and be highly ranked on residency program lists. By focusing on these outcomes, I hope to help ease your stress and unmask some of the secrets associated with residency madness.

I've organized this guide into three main parts: residency background, candidate evaluation, and interviews. So, if your applications are due tomorrow or your first interview is this week, skip to the appropriate section. The advice found in this book is the culmination of my own personal experiences as well as the opinions and experiences of numerous residency program directors, preceptors, and residents. Other than my involvement in training residents and periodically paying an overdue membership fee when needing to attend a conference or complete continuing education, I am not directly affiliated with ASHP. As you read through the coming pages, keep in mind that I tend to place high value on conversational brevity over formal verbosity.

TABLE OF CONTENTS

Section 1: Residency Background 1
    Residency Overview 3
    Benefits 6
    Application Process 8
    Timeline and Key Dates 11

Section 2: Candidate Evaluation 13
    CV 14
    Academics 16
    Work Experience 19
    Awards and Honors 20
    Leadership 21
    Research, Posters, and Publications 22
    APPE Rotations 23
    Certificates 26
    Service 27
    Letter of Intent 28
    Letters of Recommendation 30
    Midyear 33
    Social Media 37

Section 3: Interviews 40
    Interview Day 40
    Interview Sessions 43
    Practice Interview Questions 45

 Example Questions: Traditional 46
 Example Questions: Behavioral 60
 Example Questions: Unique 62
 The Most Dreaded Question 66
 Clinical Case 68
 Lunch with Current Residents 69
 Presentation 71
 Check Out 73
 Post-Interview 74
 Rank Order Lists 76
 Virtual Interviews 78

Closing 83
 Advice From Others 83
 Final Remarks 88

Bibliography 91

Appendix 97
 Appendix 1: Sample Residency Program
  Comparison Chart 97
 Appendix 2: Sample Residency Candidate
  Self-Evaluation 99

About the Author 101

SECTION 1

RESIDENCY BACKGROUND

Over the last 10 years, the landscape and competitiveness of obtaining a pharmacy residency position has changed dramatically. According to the most recent data available from ASHP, the total number of unmatched PGY1 and PGY2 applicants increased from 1,614 in 2013 to 2,596 in 2020 (1). While the number of available positions increased 53% during that time period, the number of applicants outpaced that growth and increased 64% (2,3). It's important to remember when looking at the match rates that ASHP added Phase 2 of the Match in 2016, which resulted in the PGY1 match rate peaking at 68%. Since that time, the match rate has decreased each year, bottoming out at 63% in 2020. If you consider the yearly graduating pharmacy class around the country, which has been between 14,500-15,000 students each of the last 5 years, and the 3,924 PGY1 and PGY1/PGY2 open positions in 2020, you can expect that only one quarter of each graduating class will match for residency (not even including pharmacists applying and re-applying post-graduation) (2,4). To that point, about 20% of the candidates I work with currently have already completed their PharmD degree and continue to seek post-graduate training.

| 1

With a shrinking job market and increased demand for residency training, students have now begun to build their residency application portfolios at the very beginning of pharmacy school. Because of this, the standard has now shifted towards needing to hold an organizational leadership position, interning at a hospital, and completing a pharmacy research project with poster presentation, and that's just to be competitive. Only 10-15 years ago, when myself and colleagues were applying, our applications would be dwarfed by today's average student. As was so often the case, we waited until the last minute to even consider applying for residency. I even wasn't really sure I wanted to do a residency until my ambulatory care APPE. When looking back at my pre-residency curriculum vitae (CV), I see an astoundingly average application by today's standards: 3.4 GPA at a top pharmacy school, retail pharmacy summer internship, president position in a small organization, and undergraduate clinical research; conspicuously missing hospital experience, major awards, specialty certificates, or any pharmacy-related research, posters, or publications. Using my current residency application screening tool, I would estimate my chances of matching at best would be 50-60% (depending on the number of applications and quality of letters of intent and letters of recommendation). I do believe having strong, well-chosen references from ambulatory care pharmacists and faculty members was instrumental in my matching. While it's now commonplace to see students applying to upwards of 20 programs, around a decade ago, my peers were applying to only a handful. When I was reviewing residency programs for myself, I chose to stay in a limited geographical area and focused on my ambulatory care interest: I applied to a mere two programs. After interviewing, I ended up ranking a single program, which is absolutely unheard of today. Fortunately, I did end up matching with that program; I don't recommend this strategy today (unless, of course, your heart is set on one particular program AND you have a great backup plan). If you can, use this opportunity to expand your horizons to a new city.

RESIDENCY OVERVIEW

If you weren't sure, pharmacy residency is a post graduate training program you can complete as a licensed pharmacist under the supervision and guidance of a residency program director (RPD). While these residency programs are most commonly completed immediately after obtaining your PharmD degree, it's not entirely uncommon to "go back" for residency training after already working as a pharmacist. The purpose of these programs is to build upon your PharmD, enhance your clinical experience and professional skills, and prepare you for a clinical pharmacist position (5). Residency programs are typically 12 months in duration. At this time, they include post graduate year 1 (PGY1), post graduate year 2 (PGY2), and combined PGY1/PGY2 programs. Note that completion of a PGY1 is required before PGY2 training. For those who have significant clinical experience without residency training, you may apply to waive the PGY1 requirement and apply for PGY2 training (6). PGY1 programs are designed to allow you to receive a wide range of clinical experiences, whereas PGY2 programs focus on a specialized area of practice. Below is a list of the current types of residency programs offered in collaboration with ASHP (7).

PGY1 specialties:

- Pharmacy
- Community-based pharmacy
- Managed care pharmacy

PGY1/PGY2 combined program specialties:

- Health system pharmacy administration and leadership
- Medication-use safety and policy
- Pharmacotherapy
- Pharmacy informatics
- Investigational drugs and research

PGY2 specialties:

- Ambulatory care
- Cardiology
- Corporate pharmacy leadership
- Critical care
- Emergency medicine
- Geriatrics
- Health system pharmacy administration and leadership
- Infectious disease
- Informatics
- Internal medicine
- Investigational drugs and research
- Medication-use safety and policy
- Neurology
- Nutrition support
- Oncology
- Palliative care/pain management
- Pediatrics
- Pharmacogenomics
- Pharmacotherapy
- Pharmacy outcomes/healthcare analytics
- Psychiatry
- Solid organ transplant
- Specialty pharmacy administration and leadership

General pharmacy programs account for 87% of all PGY1 programs and are offered within comprehensive hospital health-systems, which include both the inpatient and outpatient settings (7). Community-based pharmacy programs (10% of PGY1 programs) focus on outpatient settings in retail, hospital clinics, and physician offices. Finally, managed care pharmacy programs (3% of PGY1 programs) are within managed care organizations (HMOs, PPOs, and PBMs for example) (7). For the purpose of this review, we'll focus on the most common type of general pharmacy PGY1 programs. When completing a residency, expect to spend 50-60 hours (maximum 80) per week at the hospital, including perhaps every other weekend. You will have several required rotations, also known as learning experiences. These rotations may be a month in duration or longitudinal (lasting several months to the entire year). You will have inpatient staffing and clinical duties, plus the opportunity for specialized training that varies from program to program. In addition, you can choose elective rotations based on your interests and goals, such as ambulatory care, cardiology, pediatrics, infectious disease, and critical care, to name a few. It's similar to the variety of APPE rotations you can experience, except as a licensed pharmacist your scope of practice will be much greater. You'll be tasked with several projects throughout the year, including a year long research project that you will present at a conference and submit a manuscript of publishable quality. Your RPD will have oversight in your career development and in ensuring you meet the goals and objectives of your residency year. In addition, you will be trained by and have mentor preceptors that have advanced training and specialization. Your residency year, or years, will be physically, mentally, and emotionally challenging; however, once you receive your residency certificate of completion, you'll look back and be amazed by how much you have grown both professionally and personally.

Pharmacy residency programs can be ASHP-accredited (pre-candidate, candidate, or full accreditation) or non-accredited. Programs that are accredited undergo rigorous initial, annual, and reaccreditation reviews by ASHP (8). Pre-candidate status programs are newer programs that haven't yet recruited their first resident. Candidate status programs are those that have at least one resident in training but haven't yet gone through an ASHP initial accreditation survey. I wouldn't be wary of applying to these pre-candidate and candidate status programs: ASHP surveyors work with each program to ensure residency sites and experiences align with expected standards. For example, RPDs and preceptors are required to meet minimum skills and qualifications, and residents must work towards achieving mandatory educational goals and objectives. Accredited programs are those that have been approved by ASHP to meet specific, objective standards. These standards are applied to all programs, with variances for different specialties, and are updated regularly. Non-accredited residency programs can be as rigorous and rewarding as accredited programs; however, they aren't independently reviewed by ASHP for standardization or best practices. Additionally, ASHP PGY2 programs require completion of an ASHP-accredited PGY1 program, and many fulltime positions require proof of completion of an ASHP-accredited residency for employment. For the purpose of this guide, we'll assume you're pursuing a program undergoing accreditation or is currently ASHP-accredited.

BENEFITS

Often, I hear students say, "I've been in school for so long, I don't want to do another year or two of residency." My response is to remember that, while one or two extra years seem may seem daunting now, that additional training will significantly impact the trajectory of your entire career. Residency is also a great opportunity to live in a new city for a year, knowing that you can always move again when residency is over. That said, I lived an hour and half from my new bride during residency; I definitely would advise you to bring your partner with you if you decide to move, for moral support and to avoid traveling distractions.

The short- and long-term benefits of completing a residency program are pretty numerous. Benefits offered during residency vary from program to program but often include a salary range of $45,000-$55,000 (depending on specialty and location), health insurance, paid time off, meal discounts, parking, laptop, electronic and physical library access, monogrammed lab coat and scrubs, BLS and ACLS certification, live continuing education, professional pharmacy organization membership, and paid conference attendance (7). Most programs will cover the cost of attending a state-level pharmacy conference, ASHP Midyear, and a third conference to present your resident research project. Highly sought after PGY2 candidates may even be able to leverage another conference geared towards BPS certification or their specialty focus. Further, benefits of individual programs can be found on the *ASHP Online Residency Directory*, as well as each program's own website.

Over the last 5 years, almost 15,000 graduates have earned PharmD degrees each year; this was under 12,000 when I graduated in 2011 (4). Looking to the future, the U.S. Bureau of Labor Statistics estimates little to no growth in pharmacist jobs between 2018 and 2028 (9). Retail pharmacist positions are expected to decrease by 9,000 (-5.1%), while clinical positions are projected to increase by 5,100 over that time span. If you're interested in more detailed and location specific analysis, refer to the "Pharmacy Demand Report" published by Pharmacy Workforce Center (10). Regional, state, and metropolitan specific information is updated quarterly with reports of the total number and types of pharmacist job postings. Looking at Florida, for example, as of October 2019 there were 37,366 licensed pharmacists with 994 pharmacist job postings in 2019 and 530 job postings in the first half of 2020. Overall, there were 14,437 pharmacist job postings in 2019 throughout the U.S. Compare this to the 545,628 licensed pharmacists, including the new graduates and over 4,000 residency graduates actively seeking employment, and the outlook looks grim.

It's been estimated that 1-2 years of residency training is equivalent to 3-5 years of practice experience, given the extended hours worked and exposure to multiple specialty clinical roles (11). Residency allows you to explore and expand upon APPE rotations as a practicing pharmacist. This affords you the opportunity to further determine your desired practice areas and perhaps more importantly, rule out those you want to avoid. Residency also provides you with built in mentors, namely your RPD, preceptors, and non-preceptor pharmacists. In a time when pharmacist job growth is at a standstill, employers have the luxury of requiring residency training as a minimum requirement for entry level job opportunities. Additionally, residency training significantly reduces the practice experience required for student and resident precepting and board certification.

APPLICATION PROCESS

ASHP residency programs, both accredited and seeking accreditation, can be found on the *ASHP Online Residency Directory* website (7). On this site, you can filter by program type, specialty, location, and other desired parameters. The program listings include application requirements and due dates, residency program and director of pharmacy contact information, National Matching Services codes, program descriptions, and unique benefits. Requirements will typically include CV, letter of intent, three letters of recommendation, and official transcripts. It's imperative to also explore individual program sites which are linked within the directory listing, for more specific information on learning experiences, preceptors, current and past residents, and hospital services. Don't forget to consider staffing and weekend requirements, required and elective rotations offered, code coverage duties, BLS and ACLS training, and teaching certificate programs. My best advice is to create a spreadsheet, written or electronic, to track and compare your programs of interest. The most organized students I work with create a master list of programs they're interested in with application requirements, deadlines, required and elective rotations, salary, benefits, notes from speaking with residents, and comments after each interview (Appendix 1). This is especially helpful when you're applying to and interviewing with numerous programs.

To complete a pharmacy residency application, signing up for the "Pharmacy Online Residency Centralized Application Service" (PhORCAS) is required (12). PhORCAS is a service that allows you to provide personal information, upload your CV and letters of intent, and request letters of recommendation and official transcripts. There's a flat fee for the first four programs you apply to ($110 in 2019-20) and an extra fee for each additional program ($43 in 2019-20). Consider these added costs when determining the number of programs you'll apply to. If you consider skipping Midyear or attend only free networking events, that cost savings could assist you in applying to more programs (and increase your chances at matching). Luckily, with Midyear virtual and free for student ASHP members in 2020, you can benefit from not having to pay for conference attendance, hotel stay, or travel.

The "Match" is the required matching program used by ASHP and administered by the National Matching Service Inc (13). This is where rank order lists are submitted by candidates and programs after interviews are completed; imagine a secret super computer that reviews and tabulates the lists of programs and candidates to generate results of who likes whom. Of course, a flat fee is also required for this service ($160 for 2020-21). If you're keeping track, that's $270 to apply to up to four programs and $43 for each additional application thereafter. That's $958 for 20 programs!

After submitting your final application materials through PhORCAS, interview invitations will be sent out in the next couple of weeks. Programs will typically contact you with a list of available onsite (or virtual) interviews dates for you to review and submit your preference. For example, "We will be conducting interviews on 1/20, 1/27, 2/2, 2/5, and 2/10. Please respond back with your preference of dates in order." If you receive multiple interview invitations, you may not have availability to attend each one simply due to limited number of days. However, if you wait too long to respond, your preferred dates may be filled by other candidates. The best advice I can provide is to accept every offer you get as soon as possible and then deal with conflicts as they arrive. Often, programs will send out interview invitations and hold back on sending rejections. If they receive interview declines, the next candidate on the list may be invited. As challenging as it may be, don't focus on rejections or silence, but begin preparing for the interviews you have already been offered. I would also advise against reaching out to programs you haven't heard back from yet. Either they haven't decided on candidates, or you're unlikely to receive good news. Whichever the case may be, sending a follow up email will do nothing but show your impatience. Fortunately, with a compressed schedule, you shouldn't be waiting too long to find out. You can also rely on your network of peers to keep track of which programs have sent out invitations and when: most years there is a master spreadsheet file created online that students update after every invitation or rejection they receive. If you have "read it" before, share these updates by directing your fellow students to the unnamed site.

> *AnecDose: After sending out interview dates and receiving date preferences, I had a candidate reach back out. She wanted to change dates so that she could attend another interview... While I know candidates will have multiple interviews and I certainly encourage them to learn about as many programs as possible, asking about changing dates to interview elsewhere tells me you're more interested in another program than mine. Even if you applied to a program that you find only mildly interesting, you want everyone to think that they are your top choice.*

TIMELINE AND KEY DATES

The exact Match timeline is updated every year, but generally the schedule is as follows (2020-21 dates in parentheses). Refer to the schedule of dates on the National Matching Services website for updates (14).

- Register for PhORCAS and the Match in November/December (Nov 3 – Dec 31, 2020)
- Applications due in early January (Program specific, target Jan 1, 2021)
- Interviews conducted in January/February
- Phase 1 rank order list due late February/early March (March 5, 2021)
- Phase 1 Match results are released mid-March (March 19, 2021)

After the Match results are released, a list of unmatched program positions becomes available. If you didn't match in Phase 1, now is when you can apply for Phase 2. You will again need to submit applications to your desired programs through PhORCAS. Luckily, most of your materials should already be ready to go, you will just need to update your letters of intent. This process is a little more streamlined and follows a similar yearly schedule:

- Applications due in mid- to late March
- Interviews are conducted in late March and early April
- Phase 2 rank order list due early April (April 7, 2021)
- Phase 2 Match results released mid-April (April 14, 2021)

Finally, positions still available after Phase 2 become available for the "scramble," and programs can interview candidates and offer positions outside of the traditional Match process.

SECTION 2

CANDIDATE EVALUATION

Most programs will score candidate applications based on CV experiences (Appendix 2), letter of intent, and professional recommendations using clearly defined program-specific criteria. That's because ASHP sets requirements for the selection of residents that all programs must follow (5):

> Standard 1.1: "The residency program director or designee must evaluate the qualifications of applicants to pharmacy residencies through a documented, formal, procedure based on predetermined criteria."

> Standard 1.2: "The predetermined criteria and procedure used to evaluate applicants' qualifications must be used by all involved in the evaluation and ranking of applicants."

In this section, we'll review the common evaluation components of each category to make sure you score as highly as possible while standing out from the crowd. You don't have to achieve a perfect score in each category; instead, focus on improving in as many areas as you can. If you're still early in your pharmacy education, use these tips to guide your extracurricular activities now to avoid panicking when you sit down to submit applications. If you're currently preparing to apply for residency, highlight these sections if you can, but remember, it's never too late to bolster your portfolio. If you're a practicing pharmacist and want to go back for residency training, you can still use this guide to help build and strengthen your candidacy, while also gaining practical experience.

CV

Your CV will be evaluated for both formatting and content. More specifically, content includes academics, work experience, awards, leadership, research, and APPE rotations. If you take nothing else from this section, put on your calendar to update your CV at least quarterly and then monthly during rotations. Add every presentation, volunteer experience, job shadowing, or any other extracurricular completed during pharmacy school. If you wait until the end of each year or sit down to write your CV right before the application deadline, you will unquestionably forget valuable experiences.

When reviewing applications, I may not actively read every single word on your CV. However, inconsistent formatting and typos will stand out like a blue oxycodone amongst a sea of white potassium chloride tablets. Scrupulously check your margins, spacing, font, and sizing. If you currently have a CV, you know the pain of maddeningly spacing and back spacing to try to align every bit of text. To work around this and make your life infinitely easier, use a table with invisible borders for effortless formatting. Print out your CV to help check for further inconsistencies. While it's important to stand out, your CV isn't the best outlet to express your creativity; stick to standard font choices like Calibri, Arial, or Times New Roman. I definitely remember the applicants who used bold font choices, unusual formatting, and bright colors, but it probably isn't the way they wanted to be remembered. The most common question I receive relates to how to order your experiences. There is no one size fits all, so order the sections to showcase what is great about you! I would still recommend you put individual experiences in reverse chronological order. Personally, I put education first and follow the order below. Just remember the overall aesthetic and content are always of the utmost importance.

- Education
- Licensure and Certifications
- Work Experience
- APPE Rotations
- IPPE Rotations
- Research
- Posters and Presentations
- Professional Membership and Leadership
- Awards and Honors
- Service

Make sure to include your name, address, and contact information at the top of page one. For subsequent pages, put the page number and your last name in the footer. Personal statements and putting "references available upon request" are extraneous: your letter of intent will contain a more expansive version of a personal statement, and everyone knows references are available upon request (especially for residency, as you're required to provide your references through PhORCAS anyway). One common problem is having descriptions that are basically nonexistent or ones that are de facto novels. If you list that you had a critical care APPE with no description, that means very little to a reviewer: What did you do? Sit at the nurses' station in the ICU? Saved lives on rounds by recalling an obscure drug fact? Assist with code blue pharmacy response? On the other hand, if you write an overly-lengthy description, I'm probably not even going to attempt to read it. For every work and rotation experience, list 2-3 major responsibilities; paragraph or bullet point format is acceptable.

> *AnecDose: Don't try to pull a "Legally Blonde!" I've received a bright, neon pink CV. Your experience and accomplishments should speak for themselves. If you need to grab attention with a gimmick like neon paper or a bizarre font, you may be trying to hide the fact that you are not really a great candidate. While it may seem boring, with formatting, classic and professional is always the way to go.*

ACADEMICS

Your academic history will be reviewed for the strength of your pharmacy program, GPA, and any additional advanced degrees. Flawed as they may be, pharmacy school rankings are published on an annual basis, resulting in the potential for not all pharmacy degrees being equal. Specifically, the U.S. and News & World Report's methodology for ranking pharmacy schools is reported to be "based solely on the results of peer assessment surveys sent to deans, other administrators and/or faculty at accredited degree programs or schools in each discipline" and "respondents rated the academic quality of programs on a scale of 1 (marginal) to 5 (outstanding)" (15). They were instructed to select "don't know" if they did not have enough knowledge to rate a program". According to these parameters, programs are subjectively evaluated, with no objectivity on NAPLEX/MPJE exam pass rates, residency placement, research activities, student-faculty ratio, or anything else that would seem to characterize a strong college of pharmacy. As a result, this process inherently downgrades newer programs and consistently rewards established programs. Many seasoned pharmacists and program directors may also choose to rank accelerated programs lower than traditional four-year programs. The most common reasons for this are due to unfamiliarity with accelerated programs and the perception that students lose out on the opportunity to gain practice experience during fulltime summer internships. Regardless of your thoughts on the ranking process, the fact is they are absolutely used to score and rank candidates. If you're reading this prior to applying to pharmacy school, consider these rankings in your decision-making process. You may also want to review match results by school to help you decide on a program (16). In 2020, the top five programs with the highest number of matched PGY1 residents were the University of Florida (101), University of California-SF (81), University of North Carolina (78), University of Kentucky (75), and University of Wisconsin (71). Additionally, only five programs had an 80% match rate with 50 or more students submitting rank order lists: University of California-SF (90%), University of North Carolina (83%), University of Texas-Austin (82%), University of Wisconsin (82%), and University of Missouri-KC (82%).

Unsurprisingly, GPA is also incorporated into your academic evaluation. While a 4.0 GPA will not guarantee residency interviews, competitive programs that receive a high volume of applications may use a GPA cutoff to help whittle down the number of applications they fully review. I've seen cutoffs of 3.0

and 3.2 used in practice or automatically eliminating those with any D's or F's. Fortunately, APPE rotations can be expected to increase your GPA, unless of course your program's rotations are pass/fail. Remember that GPA is only one part of the application review. A perfect GPA without any extracurriculars raises red flags about leadership and the ability to multitask. In fact, if a student struggles their first year and rebounds to attain high marks, be active on campus, and maintain an internship, at least I know they have the ability to face adversity and improve. Of course, that's coming from someone who pulled multiple C's in his P1 year. Wherever your GPA currently sits, don't set a potentially unrealistic goal of bringing it up to a 4.0. If your GPA is 3.4, set a more achievable overall goal for the next semester, of >3.5 or all B+ grades or higher, for instance.

Finally, one great way to score highly in this category is to have a complementary advanced degree. While not the norm, it's becoming more common to review candidates who have a Master of Business Administration (MBA) or Master of Public Health (MPH) degree. Whether these are completed prior to, concomitantly, or after pharmacy school, it's valuable experience, nonetheless. As an ambulatory care pharmacist, experience with return on investment, SWOT analysis, proposals, and business planning is paramount to expanding clinical pharmacy services and establishing new clinics. As the field of population health booms, holding an MPH degree could have significant practical implications. With the expansion of available online degree programs, the opportunity is there to complete these additional degrees during pharmacy school or post-graduation in anticipation of re-applying to residency programs. Administration and leadership residencies certainly recognize the benefits of additional education, with many offering Master's degrees as part of residency training. If pharmacy is your second degree or you had the ability to complete a dual degree, make sure to highlight these strengths and how they can help you be a better resident and pharmacist in your letter of intent and during interviews.

WORK EXPERIENCE

As you may know, many of your classmates will have a wide range of job experience, or some may have chosen not to work during school. Evaluating and scoring various employments can be challenging, particularly for candidates with significant non-pharmacy experience or previous careers. In simply complicated terms, the longer you work the better, and hospital experience is better than retail which is better than non-pharmacy positions. If you're currently in your final year of pharmacy school and on APPE rotations, it will be too late to change your work experience. However, in P1, P2, and P3 years, I would recommend that you put significant energy into obtaining a hospital internship. Even volunteering on the weekends is valuable experience and may lead to an internship in the future. Not only could you gain clinical and intravenous preparation experience, but learning an electronic medical record and automated dispensing cabinet makes for a much easier transition into residency. Furthermore, most hospitals systems that take interns will also have residency programs and would unquestionably prefer to keep their own interns as residents. Assuming you have made a favorable impression, who wouldn't want a pre-trained candidate who already knows the system and is ready to build on that knowledge? I've even seen an intern be the main candidate for a residency program that hadn't even been created yet. These internships can give you an inside track to residency programs and may provide you the confidence in applying to more competitive programs, knowing you have a safer backup option. Even if you don't have hospital experience, use your own personal work history to highlight your strengths. If you have been in retail, you can likely talk about immunizations, patient education, training other staff members, and conflict resolution. Retail and MTM work experiences can provide advantages to community-based residency programs, as well. In lieu of practical pharmacy experience, remember to list any other positions you may have held. A manager position or previous career experience can offer valuable attributes for a future pharmacist.

AWARDS AND HONORS

This is a category that admittedly doesn't get a lot of focus from programs yet is still very important. A national award from ASHP, APhA, or other pharmacy organization makes a huge statement. Recognition from a state-level organization, hospital system, or pharmacy chain is also quite valuable (including honor society induction, employee of the month, and scholarships). While more local awards and honors have less impact on your candidate scoring, make sure you double check that you haven't overlooked any recognition you have received at school or work. You can certainly report being on the Dean's List, but your GPA already takes this into account. Don't be afraid to include awards from your previous degrees: since I did not win any significant awards while in pharmacy school, I made sure to include National Chemistry Honor Society and departmental student of the year from my undergrad years.

LEADERSHIP

This section really begins and ends with holding a president or vice president position in a pharmacy organization. Whether you're the president of the Student National Pharmaceutical Association (SNPhA) or a local pharmacy club with only ten members, I'm checking a box for full points after I see anything that says president or vice president. I don't mean to minimize the value of national or state-level leadership positions but I may be reviewing 50 applications for screening purposes, so I would look at these similarly. However, these higher-level examples of leadership should be at the top of your list of accomplishments to highlight in your letter of intent and during interviews. Treasurer, secretary, historian, and chair positions score nicely, but these really pale in comparison to the big two. Organizational membership is a plus, but don't confuse membership with leadership. Anyone can pay $50-100 to join a club right before applications to artificially build up a resume. Another option that doesn't always get explored is starting a new organization. If your campus lacks a nuclear or geriatrics related club, for example, start one. Even if you can only begin the process before residency applications are due, it will show great initiative and be a talking point for your interviews.

AnecDose: Candidates have often listed membership in multiple organizations as an example of leadership with no reasonable explanation. Having minimal participation in a lot of clubs is exponentially less valuable than being invested and heavily involved in one. When I see that someone has membership in 12 groups but lacks a leadership position, I see someone trying to pad their resume without actually making an impact.

RESEARCH, POSTERS, AND PUBLICATIONS

Unfortunately, or fortunately depending on your perspective, this is an area that has become an unofficial requirement over the last 5-10 years. I was fortunate enough to be required to complete a senior research project as an undergrad, and I somehow had the unwitting foresight to complete a small randomized controlled trial (evaluating the effects of creatine and HMB supplementation on exercise performance and body composition, if you're interested). While not a pharmacy-related topic, I gained valuable experience with research proposal writing, IRB submission, conducting a placebo-controlled crossover study design, manuscript writing, and presenting results to a large audience campus-wide. If you're still a year away from residency applications, I would strongly suggest asking every faculty member, APPE preceptor, and current resident you know if you can assist with their research. Start targeting your professors by the end of your first year of pharmacy school. Then inquire with preceptors and residents, as soon as rotations begin (IPPE and especially APPE). Having multiple rotations at one site is a great opportunity to help with a longitudinal project, so keep this in mind when choosing where to sign up. Tasks as simple as data collection and background research are still valuable experiences you can bring into your PGY1 year. When evaluating this category, involvement in pharmacy clinical research is king and would maximize your potential point total. If this is unattainable, don't be discouraged. Assisting in laboratory research or non-pharmacy research projects are still reliable point generators. Moreover, presenting a poster at Midyear or any other conference will help boost your portfolio and also provides you another talking point when meeting with RPDs and residents at Midyear or during interviews. Would I be impressed if you were published in the *New England Journal of Medicine*? Absolutely, but that isn't very realistic. Target publications by ASHP, APhA, Pharmacy Times, and other pharmacy specific journals and newsletters. Many student specific periodicals publish pieces that are just based on student experiences, opinions, and advice. Be aware that if you don't take advantage of opportunities like these, your competition will certainly be submitting to those publications. Whether or not you're able to publish a paper or present a poster at a national-level, strive to publish articles at your school or even newsletters at your APPE sites.

PGY1 residents seeking PGY2 residencies will definitely be required to complete a research project of publishable quality. Consider your specialty interests when deciding on your year long research project: you don't want to be interviewing for a pediatrics PGY2 position and have your only research experience be in geriatric solid organ transplant.

APPE ROTATIONS

When choosing APPE rotations, best practice is to choose clinical, direct patient care rotations (such as hospital practice, cardiology, infectious disease, emergency medicine, oncology, and ambulatory care; non-clinical, non-direct patient care rotations may include informatics, managed care, long term care, drug information, and management) for your electives. Depending on your program and state requirements, students will have discrepancies in the number of elective rotations and rotation length. For example, if one student has four-week rotations and can take five extra months of advanced hospital practice, critical care, and trauma rotations while another has made the choice of their two six-week electives to be pharmacy industry and informatics, which would you guess is going to be more appealing to an ICU-based RPD? While the specifics and applicability of these rotations should be pertinent to your goals and interests, the overarching concept it to challenge yourself clinically with direct patient care. On the contrary, if you know you want to pursue an administrative or medication safety residency, focus on those types of rotations. If you want to complete a community-based program, it makes more sense to take retail, compounding, and MTM electives. I would urge you to discuss your choice of rotations with faculty, IPPE preceptors, and current residents. Of course, with COVID cancelling many rotations in 2020, you may not have had as many clinical or pertinent experiences as you wanted. I would expect this to be taken into consideration when programs evaluate APPE rotations as it has had a nation-wide impact. If you did have several virtual rotations, use any extra time to work on projects, publish an article, or complete certificate programs. Be sure to write descriptions of these rotations on your CV that highlight any special projects or unique experiences. Maybe you feel like at your last rotation you just created disease state outlines for a month, but you could present that as "evaluated primary literature and created evidenced-based references and tools for pharmacists and pharmacy students". Highlight any patient care activities and relate them back to the "Pharmacists' Patient Care Process" that has become the focus of experiential education in pharmacy everywhere.

For those PGY1 residents looking to continue with a PGY2, you of course want a comprehensive residency experience but it's still important to consider your specialty interests when choosing rotation electives at the beginning of your residency year. As an ambulatory care RPD, a resident with six months of ambulatory care electives is far more attractive to me than a candidate who primarily spent time in critical care learning experiences. These electives afford you the opportunity to gain important clinical and practical knowledge in specialty areas of genuine interest to you.

As you enter the final year of your professional education (or begin residency), keep in mind that rotations can serve as month-long interviews. For the majority of students, you will be applying to residency programs where you had rotations and asking those same preceptors for letters of recommendation. When I see student applications for those who had rotations at our site or in the same hospital-system, I heavily rely on the experience and opinion of their preceptors. A carefully crafted application is almost negligible compared to learning how you work and behave over the course of a rotation. Important questions I would ask your preceptor include: can you describe their level of professionalism during patient interactions? Did they do the bare minimum required or ask for additional projects to aid their learning? How are their organizational and presentation skills? Would you recommend this student for our residency program? As a student I always rolled my eyes when anyone said that pharmacy is a small world, but this cliché is absolutely true. I can remember times having run into former students 2,500 miles away from where we met and have had students with the same mentors that I had 10 years ago. My former retail pharmacy manager now works in a mail order pharmacy with several of my former classmates, and I now collaborate with several pharmacists with whom I'd once interviewed. One bad experience at a rotation site or on campus could, and likely will, invariably find the ears of your potential RPD.

AnecDose: During an interview at PPS (ASHP's Personal Placement Service), a PGY1 resident had a beautifully crafted story about why she wanted to pursue ambulatory care. It all sounded great. The problem? Her PGY1 year included just one lonely, required ambulatory care learning experience while her electives focused on critical care and infectious disease. While I want a well-rounded resident, I need to see experiences and work products that show your sincere commitment to my specialty.

CERTIFICATES

Completing additional pharmacy-related certificate programs is an easy way to add extra points to your CV score. Take warning and know the difference between a certification and a certificate. Certification is usually an earned credential based on meeting specific practice, knowledge, and experience qualification. In contrast, a certificate program is typically completion of an educational or continuing education program. While several programs are available through the major pharmacy organizations, the offerings by APhA tend to be the most affordable and ASHP has the widest variety (17,18). If you have already completed immunization and BLS training, certainly include those in your CV and application materials. But don't count on these to make you memorable, as nearly every other candidate will have completed those, too. I'm looking for candidates who go above and beyond to expand their knowledge and build towards career-long goals. If you're on an ambulatory care track, shoot for diabetes and cardiovascular certificate programs; for an inpatient focus, look into sterile compounding, medication reconciliation, or pharmacokinetics. Remember, every added experience and credential should have a benefit to your career interests and goals; there is no need to waste hundreds of dollars just to add a meaningless line on you CV.

AnecDose: I once reviewed an applicant that listed being a "Certified Diabetes Educator" despite still being in pharmacy school with no listed previous careers. Certified Diabetes Educators, now known as Certified Diabetes Care and Education Specialists, require among other standards, completion of a degree, two years of experience, and at least 1,000 hours of direct patient care. What the student had actually completed was "The Pharmacist and Patient-Centered Diabetes Care" certificate program through APhA. At best, the student was careless in documenting his experience. At worst, he was deliberately misrepresenting his qualifications.

SERVICE

Community service and involvement is a more challenging personal experience to evaluate for residency candidates. Some programs and evaluators may not specifically score this category, while others see this as an aspect of leadership. The simple solution is to list all of your service opportunities, whether they were to your community, church, school, or even friends and neighbors. However, make sure to highlight what roll you played and what you actually did. Listing multiple canned food drives under community service is a bit generic, but if you can say that you organized the event and recruited your classmates, that shows teamwork and leadership. From my perspective, I usually see that all applicants have a half to full page of community service, so there usually isn't any significant differentiation or impact from my point of view. You could benefit from discussing any unique experiences (medical mission trips, pharmacy advocacy, or disaster relieve for example) in your letter of intent and interviews. One major exception is that Veteran's Affairs residency programs may give hiring preference to Veterans and, potentially, their family. If this situation is applicable to you, thank you for your service, and please be sure to contact the Veterans Benefits Administration for more information and assistance.

LETTER OF INTENT

"I am writing to express my sincere interest in the PGY1 program offered at *<insert hospital name>*. Your program interests me due to your critical care, ambulatory care, oncology, informatics, leadership, research, and surgery rotations. I enjoyed meeting your resident at Midyear. I am a dedicated, hardworking, and compassionate student with a strong passion to help others. My goals are to complete PGY1 and PGY2 residencies, obtain board certification, and become a clinical pharmacist. I will bring leadership, ambition, and enthusiasm to your program. I look forward to meeting you and learning more about your residency program."

Are you still awake? If this sounds like your letter of intent, scrap it and start over. More than half of the letters I've read are this generic and uninspired. Yes, you need to professionally state your interest. Yes, you need to express why you're interested in the program. And yes, absolutely explain what you have to offer. No, don't just cut and paste from internet example letters. No, don't just list a bunch of random electives that are pertinent to your interests. Also, don't write generic goals. Don't use cliché personal strengths. I want to feel like I'm actually learning about an applicant through their letter. To be frank, when I'm reading letter after letter after letter, there are three main components I look for:

1) Consistent formatting, proper grammar, and leck of typos (intentional: that's distracting, right?)
2) Specificity to my program, statement of specific short- and long-term career goals, and what you have to offer my program
3) Something unique or memorable about you or your experience

When it comes down to reading letters ad nauseum, I'm honestly just going to remember anything that sets you apart from your peers, positive or negative. Again, no Comic Sans or emojis. Instead, include a personal connection to the practice of pharmacy, a special project on rotations, or a once in a lifetime patient experience that changed your perspective.

Consider this short example instead:
"I am writing to express my sincere interest in the PGY1 program offered at *<insert hospital name>*. Your program interests me due to your expanded emergency medicine pharmacy programs and option for additional critical care experiences. I enjoyed meeting your resident, *<insert name>*, at Midyear and learning about his research project on the cost-benefit analysis of pharmacists in the emergency department. After seeing my grandfather in the hospital for an acute MI and subsequent CABG, I wanted to learn as much as possible about stabilizing and treating patients with acute medical emergencies. While on APPE rotations, I have been recognized for creating engaging presentations, utilizing a pharmacy spin on common gameshows. My careers goals are to complete PGY1 and emergency medicine PGY2 residencies, obtain board certification in criti-

cal care, advocate for emergency medicine pharmacy board certification, and help establish pharmacist presence in the ER as standard of care. I will bring my experience conducting multiple research projects and my ability to perform best under stressful situations to your program. I look forward to meeting you and learning more about your residency program."

How long should these letters be? I personally prefer a one-page limit; this is merely an introduction to who you are. Keep in mind that RPDs will likely have dozens to read. Many of my colleagues don't have a strict page limit, but they definitely don't want to read anything longer than two pages. If at all possible, work with an independent pharmacist or career coach who can provide you with objective feedback. I also suggest having multiple friends, family, and preceptors review your letters. PGY1 residents, rely on your co-residents, preceptors, and RPD to read and critique your letters.

> *AnecDose: I received a letter addressed to another program. Double check, triple check, and have a friend check your letters; it's as easy to mix them up as it is to forget to attach a document to an email. Remember this example not only for residency applications but also future job applications. In a competitive job market, it only takes one small misstep such as this to prevent you from gaining employment.*

LETTERS OF RECOMMENDATION

Review the requirements of every program to which you apply very carefully. While most require three references, some may want four or have specific requests for a minimum number from faculty or preceptors. You will need to ask for letters of recommendation and then send formal requests through PhORCAS. Prime targets should be faculty, APPE preceptors, and pharmacists from where you intern. For current PGY1 residents, I would expect your letters to come from your RPD and current preceptors. If you're interested in a cardiology PGY2, make sure your cardiology preceptor is one of your references. If your RPD isn't one of your three references, I would immediately be questioning why not? Ask if they are willing to write a **favorable** recommendation. Don't wait until right before Christmas break to ask; preceptors get busy with residency applications, letters of recommendation, gaps between APPE rotations, and you know, life outside of work. Be sure to discuss your career and program interests with them so the professional reference can be pertinent to you and the individual programs to which you're applying. The recommendation process is also a bit novel compared to what you may be thinking. The reference process through PhORCAS has standardized questions. Even if we wanted to, references don't just write a one-page recommendation about how fantastic you are.

The standard recommendation form is public and available on the ASHP website (19), so use it as your cheat sheet. The form begins by asking the recommender how long they have known you, how much time you've interacted with each other, and your professional relationship. References are asked to choose if you exceed expectations for an entering resident, appropriately meet expectations for an entering resident, or fail to meet expectations for an entering resident in the following domains:

- Writing skills
- Oral communication
- Leadership and mentoring

- Organization and time management
- Teamwork
- Problem solving
- Patient interactions
- Dependability
- Independence
- Acceptance of constructive criticism
- Maturity
- Professionalism

Next, references are asked for a narrative assessment based on:

- Independence and comparison to other students
- Strengths
- Areas for Improvement (aka weaknesses)
- Fit for the specific program
- Other observations

Finally, references must choose the level for which they recommend you:

- Highly recommend
- Recommend
- Recommend with reservations
- Do not recommend

It's critical that you consider this evaluation when you're requesting recommendation letters. Truth be told, I want to see that your skills exceed expectations or are at least appropriate to an entering pharmacy resident and that your self-chosen references highly recommend you. The appearance of failing to meet expectations, being recommended with reservations, or not being recommend at all are likely to have you eliminated from the evaluation process. As preceptors, we're familiar with these questions and how applicants are evaluated. I would hope that your reference would provide honest feedback and would advise you to request another reference, if they felt unable to provide a glowing review.

MIDYEAR

As the majority of the country's population is transitioning from Thanksgiving to Christmas, the pharmacy world begins focusing on ASHP's Midyear Clinical Meeting. Let the continuing education, networking, exhibit halls, and residency showcase madness begin (20). Without hesitation, the number one question I get asked by students is if they should attend Midyear. For the majority of students, I would say no. The best parts of Midyear are traveling to a new city, hanging out with friends, compiling a bag of free swag, and perhaps attending the keynote speaker session. The main attraction for residency candidates is, you guessed it, the residency showcase. If you have never been, imagine a huge auditorium with hundreds of booths set up for a myriad of available residency programs. Each booth has several residents and the RPD or other preceptor. The entrance to the room is closed with thousands of students lined up ready to stampede through the doors: in 2019 over 7,000 students attended! As the clock strikes 8 AM and the doors are thrown open, the auditorium is filled with frenzied students and a palpable frenetic energy. There is instantly a buzzing sound that would rival a swarm of cicada and the temperature rises at least ten degrees (terrible for being in a suit). Candidates storm their preferred residency programs and aim to hurl thoughtful, engaging questions at residents and RPDs… or not. Without a doubt, the majority of interactions include questions that have answers readily found on our website or candidates awkwardly lingering around. You're way more likely to make a negative impression than a positive one. Unless you have the most intriguing, well research question in the history of the residency showcase that you must in person, you don't need to attend Midyear. Additionally, as an RPD, I honestly don't want to be there. I want my residents to speak with candidates and share their first-person experiences. What I really want to do is get some live continuing education and enjoy my free vacation to New Orleans, Anaheim, Las Vegas, or Orlando. If you do insist on attending, below are a list of do's and don'ts for the in-person showcase:

Do:

- Leave your friends behind (this should be a strictly professional endeavor)
- Target specific programs of most interest to you
- Research the programs and ask 1-2 <u>thoughtful</u> questions
- Focus on learning from the residents' experiences and insights
- Have a positive attitude
- Bring business cards (we write notes about you on the back)
- Invite us to view your poster presentation
- Thank everyone
- Write down notes immediately afterwards

Don't:

- Wander aimlessly
- Ask generic questions or those easily found online

- Linger
- Be shy
- Insist on speaking with the RPD
- Chew gum
- Bathe in cologne or perfume
- Stay out late drinking the night before

AnecDose: There are way too many examples to share, so I'll try to pick just one. Once a student came to our booth and immediately asked to speak to the RPD. He then proceeded to ask me something only the RPD could have answered: "please tell me about the program." Clearly, this wouldn't require the RPD, and I realize the program does need to have a sales pitch; however, if you ask the most common, open, generic question, I'm going to assume you have done zero research. Nonetheless, I obliged this student's request only to find he had absolutely no follow up questions. Yet he continued to hover around our booth for the next 30 minutes. AWKWARD.

AnecDose, guest edition: As a fourth-year student, I went to Midyear in Las Vegas 1) because it's Vegas and 2) for the residency showcase. Unfortunately, when the time came for Tuesday morning (when the programs I was most interested in had their showcase), I was out with food poisoning. Thankfully, I talked a friend into attending booths for me, asking thoughtful questions, and handing out my business card. I ended up matching with my top program and they "remembered" me from Midyear. I got lucky that the "other me" made a good impression, but I wouldn't recommend others choose that path for themselves.

ASHP's PPS is essentially a large recruitment and interview session held at Midyear (21). It's primarily intended for full time job opportunities, PGY2 programs, and combined PGY1/PGY2 programs. You have the ability to schedule one on one time with hiring managers and directors. From my experience, these "interviews" are essentially information gathering sessions or pre-interviews. For residency positions, you will still be required to apply through PhORCAS and participate in full onsite (or virtual) interviews. Even interviews for full time positions will more than likely still require you to complete the full application process and extensive interviews post-PPS. As an RPD at these sessions, my main goal was to share insights about our program individually with candidates to hopefully increase the number of applications we received. For the majority of candidates, the cost of attending PPS does not seem worthwhile merely for one on one information sessions. If you're interested in learning more about the types of positions listed above and cost isn't a factor, then it might be worth your time. The interview sessions are scheduled in 30-minute intervals but it's recommended to avoid scheduling back to back spots, in case you run over time talking to a program you really like. Also consider that the walk from one booth to another may take you several minutes: give yourself ample time, to decrease stress. You should also check the map and walk the room ahead of time to ensure you know where you need to go. Furthermore, even without registering for the PPS, you may have the opportunity to meet with those programs at other events at Midyear or online.

With Midyear being virtual and free for student and resident ASHP members in 2020, the exact ensuing experience is unknown, as of this writing (20). But it's always true that virtual events or open houses serve as a good forum for programs to give presentations and overviews about their residency. They aren't intended for significant one on one interaction. However, if you can attend for free and learn more about programs, go for it! Just don't expect to have private conversations with residents and RPDs. In group Q&A sessions, you may be able to benefit from hearing other student questions without having to muster up the courage to ask yourself. From a program perspective, I'm not expecting to see many candidates face to face, and again, I would have the intention of drumming up interest in and applications for my residency positions. For a more intimate experience, consider attending local residency forums at your college or pharmacy or through your local pharmacy organizations.

SOCIAL MEDIA

The controversy of social media professionalism may have peaked in the summer of 2020 with a publication that sought to evaluate the unprofessional social media behavior of young vascular surgeons (20). Specifically, the classification of bikini/swimwear as "inappropriate attire" resulted in a backlash of physicians (amongst others) posting swimsuit pictures in protest. The article was subsequently retracted; however, the issues of gender equality and who defines the line of professionalism in our personal yet public lives, remain unaddressed or unanswered by our profession at large.

The hard truth is, RPDs may be viewing your social media accounts. Surveys have shown that up to 28% of pharmacy RPDs viewed a candidate's social media, and 89% agreed that anything freely published online was fair to help judge a candidate's professionalism and character (23,24). While another survey showed only 17% of medical RPDs checked social media for candidate insight, over a third of those reported ranking candidates lower based on what they found (25).

In an age where we all spend too much time on Facebook, Instagram, TikTok, Twitter, and a multitude of other platforms (forgive me if I missed any other popular platforms, I'm approaching my late-30s), it's far too easy to overshare. While we all have the freedom to post whatever we want, others have the same freedom to react to and interpreter what you posted. As you transition into being a working professional, you may be seen as representing your employer when you post content online.

Continuing our look at social media, I think you can characterize the platforms into professional and non-professional domains. If you're posting on LinkedIn, for example, the expected level of professionalism is a lot higher than SnapChat or Tumblr. You can browse an endless amount of LinkedIn profiles for pretty standard and consistent profiles: profile picture is a headshot in professional attire with or without lab coat, brief about me section with career goals or previous experience, and a list of current and past job titles. Don't overthink it, I look at these sites as a place to network and keep up to date on career-related news not an outlet to overly express your personality. On the other hand, the other social media platforms are a bit of the wild west, perhaps with pictures going back to your high school and college days. Considering your privacy settings is the first step in protecting yourself. Second, review your previous posts and pictures. I really don't care if you have a good time outside of work (or dare I say, you're a Yankees fan). It makes no difference to me your religious beliefs, political stance, or sexual orientation, but if you express violence, hate speech, or aggression, it may result in employers questioning your ability to work in a diverse medical center or how you might react when your recommendations aren't accepted by providers. Most of all, remember the standards and expectations of our profession. HIPAA violations, driving under the influence, or illegal substance use could result in disciplinary actions by your Board of Pharmacy, and I would use that same minimum standard for potential residency screening. Ultimately, as an adult and professional, it's up to you to determine what is acceptable to voluntarily publish online. Finally, consider that RPDs for 2,614 programs may have 2,614 different viewpoints.

SECTION 3

INTERVIEWS

INTERVIEW DAY

The day has arrived! The last couple months, years really, have been building up to this moment. The next couple hours could make or break the next 40 years of your career. Enough pressure? Whenever I go to interviews, I always ask myself, "What's the worst thing that could happen? What do I have to lose?" If you totally bomb an interview, move on, you probably won't see any of those people again, and you have plenty of other interviews ahead of you. As an RPD or preceptor, even if your interview isn't going well, I'm not going to call you out on it. We have all been in your shoes before and, believe it or not, we really do want you to do well.

Whether you're traveling locally or across country, you can never be too cautious in arriving to the right place at the right time. If traveling, it's best to arrive at least the day before to scope out the location you will be interviewing. There's not much worse than arriving to the correct site on time, but then frantically looking for the right parking lot or running around searching for the actual meetup location. Even if you're interviewing locally, make sure you stake out the site before you're sprinting up flights of stairs in the least comfortable clothes you own.

Interviews are going to be stressful; this is true for candidates and programs alike. I would strongly suggest taking the morning to help de-pressurize yourself. For me, I'll wake up early and hit the gym or go for a run. For you, it may be just taking your dog for a walk, yoga, playing a game, reading, or just putting on some mindless tv. Spend five minutes reviewing the program's website, especially if you will be interviewing with multiple programs. Now isn't the time to eat new adventurous foods, stick to what you normally eat every day that you know won't upset your stomach. Dust off your most professional attire and make sure everything is clean and ironed. If you don't know how to use an iron, ask a friend or spend a few minutes on YouTube. It's a good idea to bring a second set of dress clothes too; I'm a strong believer in being overprepared. As an interviewer, I definitely wouldn't mark someone down for spilling coffee on themselves, everyone has done it. However, as the interviewee, feeling sharp and cleaned up is going to help boost your confidence. So, pack up your notebook, CV, business cards, and most importantly a positive attitude and head off to face the day with these tips. Remember to account for traffic, and leave even earlier than you think you should. Better to be early and wait around than driving 80 mph through a hospital parking lot.

AnecDose: A candidate who lived less than 30 minutes from the residency site showed up two hours late for the interview, citing bad traffic for the delay. As far as we were aware, there were no major backup delays reported on the interstate. There are certainly times where circumstances are outside of your control (a complete highway shutdown, your tire blows out, an unexpected blizzard) but don't start your interview with fabricated excuses. Needless to say, that candidate did not make the rank order list.

While specifics of the day (or half day) will vary from program to program, we'll follow the sample interview schedule below.

	Welcome and program overview with RPD
	Interview with RPD
	Interview with preceptors
	Interview with leadership
	Clinical patient case review
	Tour and lunch with current residents
	Formal presentation
	Wrap up and final Q&A with RPD

Now that you've arrived in the right building, at the right time, the day can officially begin. Expect to show up at the meeting spot with other candidates, could be 2-3, or upwards of 10 or more. You may see the top student in your class or one that already interns at the residency site. You can't control other candidates, how they interview, or what the program is looking for. You can only control yourself; don't dwell on your competition. Your objectives are all that matter: 1) to learn about the residency program and 2) to build rapport with the RPD, preceptors, and residents.

After the RPD or current residents meet you for an informal greeting, it's time to learn about the program. When I conducted program overviews, I used presentation slides to introduce myself, review the plan for the day, and walk through the program specifics (requirements, learning experiences, electives, benefits, hospital policies, etc.). My goal is to help you understand what we offer and increase your interest in our program. The truth is, I'm feeling the same nerves as you are, so I'm probably trying to ease the tension along the way by incorporating a corny joke (please respond with a pity laugh). Questions are certainly encouraged, as they give me a first impression on who is prepared. I'm also observing how you interact with myself and other candidates.

INTERVIEW SESSIONS

Next, we move on to the dreaded question and answer interviews. Your application materials got you this far, but how you interview will determine whether or not you match. My programs have usually had candidates interview one on one with the RPD, a panel of preceptors, and leadership (either the director of pharmacy, clinical coordinator, or RPDs from our other residency programs). For most sessions, expect to be asked to first introduce yourself, followed by a set of standard questions, and finally the chance for you to ask us questions. As hard as it may be to believe, there are three facts you should accept heading into these meetings. First, interviewers are also nervous. Meeting new people taxes my introverted soul, and I also have to consider that students or PGY1s may frankly not be interested in our program. I don't want to have unfilled positions and have to go through Phase 2 of the Match or the scramble. We may be experienced pharmacists, but you never forget the anxiety of being a student and the terror of residency interviews. Second, we really just want to get to know you to see if we're a fit for one another. I would take a candidate that has career goals and interests that align with our program over a straight-A student that aspires to specialize in an area we don't offer. Finally, RPDs and preceptors are actually all just regular people with outside lives. You may see an intimidating presence with a library's worth of publications and seemingly the entire alphabet of certifications after their name; however, that same person has a personal life and even interests outside of pharmacy. Oftentimes when I do mock interviews online, I'll show up wearing a hat and hoodie, show off my corgi, "Toast," on camera, and talk about hiking in the Smoky Mountains to help remind candidates of exactly that point.

When answering questions, remember these are open-ended questions, so a simple "yes" or "no" will not suffice. On the other hand, if your response goes on for too long, I'll start zoning out about last night's football game or what's for lunch. I suggest you target 1-2 minute answer responses. This doesn't mean you should memorize a scripted answer for every known interview question. Instead, you need to practice giving conversational responses and engaging in back and forth dialogue with the interviewer. So, how do you practice answering questions without sounding too scripted? Do I practice in front of the mirror? Do I talk to my dog? The two most effective strategies I've found are mock interviews with someone you don't know very well (to simulate the formal interview environment) and also practicing with a close friend or relative to help guide you in a more conversational tone. It's unlikely that you'd give a robotically recited answer to your best friend, spouse, or parent. Furthermore, multiple studies have actually shown that pharmacy students who engaged in mock interview sessions match at a significantly higher rate, upwards of 83% (26-28).

If you get asked a question that you cannot immediately answer, feel free to ask for clarification or repeat back the question to buy yourself a bit more time. Remember, it's better to pause and formulate a coherent response than to jump into a thoughtless answer. As an RPD, in addition to the content of what you say, I'm also considering how you communicate. Can you look us in the eye? Can you sit still without nervously fidgeting? And most importantly, are you excited for the opportunity or are you absolutely miserable? SMILE. It doesn't have to be an ear-to-ear over the top smile. I don't need to see your fillings and molars, but a friendly grin to show that you don't absolutely hate talking about my residency program will go a long way. See below for practice interview questions and answers. Lastly, at the conclusion of each interview session, always thank everyone for their time and consideration.

> *AnecDose: I remember starting an interview by asking a candidate to tell me about herself. Fifteen minutes later, I forgot what question I even asked and couldn't recall anything she said. Residency will be full of challenges to your time management skills; if you can't effectively manage your time in this scenario, I wouldn't feel confident you could do it while you're in my program. Keep it concise!*

PRACTICE INTERVIEW QUESTIONS

I polled a group of students on whether they would prefer a list of hundreds of practice questions or a shorter list of questions with tips on how to answer; the overwhelming majority wanted an in depth and quality review over quantity. In homage to the overall 63% match rate for PGY1 in 2020, you will find 63 interview questions with answering strategies or sample responses. Remember these are just a sample of hundreds of potential questions, each with varying possible permutations and spinoffs. Questions are broken down into the following classifications: standard, behavioral, and unique. Certainly, there are innumerable practice questions, but the most important thing is to actually practice. Remember, that does not mean rote memorization of how you would answer questions, but actual practice. You're not learning answers, but how to answer. You may never become the most charmingly engaging interviewee, but no matter where you are today, you can improve. Interview skills will continue to develop over the years but will only be fortified with conscious practice. I can't stress these points enough; ask a friend or family member to turn on the interrogation light and grill you with questions. Even better, preceptors or residents at your APPE sites sometimes provide workshops to more accurately replicate the interview question and answer sessions.

EXAMPLE QUESTIONS: TRADITIONAL

1. Tell me about yourself
   This is by far the most common opening question and your opportunity to say whatever is most important for you to express. A general template should include where you're from, your pharmacy school, why you're becoming a pharmacist, and anything unique about you or your experiences. Have you worked on a pharmacy related clinical trial or research project? Did you start a new pharmacy organization? Do you participate in medical mission trips? Was someone in your family (or yourself) affected by a chronic or

acute illness that required medication therapy that piqued your interest in the profession? Imagine that this answer is the only thing that is remembered from your interview. It's almost guaranteed this question will be asked during your interviews, likely more than once. I know it can be overwhelming to try and summarize your entire existence into 1-2 minutes, so practice your response to this question, and others; but always make sure to answer in a conversational manner, not a recited speech.

2. Why did you decide to become a pharmacist?
   It can be a great benefit to have a unique personal connection to pharmacy similar to the above question. The standard answers of wanting to help people or being interested in math and science are sadly forgettable. Use a specific example from your life and make it memorable. When I hear a story about someone watching their grandparent struggle with diabetes, for example, I know that candidate is really invested in pharmacy and helping others. If you're applying to PGY2 programs, tell me specifically why you're interested in the specialty: if you're wanting another year of residency life, you surely have a powerful reason.

3. Why do you want to do a residency?
   You may be thinking "because I don't know what else to do" or "I don't want to do retail." This is a good time to avoid being overly blunt. Discuss how clinically trained pharmacists can push our profession to new heights and your desire to specialize in a certain area of practice. Perhaps you have friends already in residency, so you could talk about the experiences

they've shared that you want for your life. Or maybe it was an outstanding IPPE/APPE or preceptor who sparked your curiosity and pushed you to lean more. This question will require some introspection to really determine what it is that drives you.

4. Why are you interested in this particular program?
Do research and give specific examples that are unique to each program. For example, discuss rotation options, previous research publications, PGY2 programs, previous interactions with their residents, their preceptors, or their RPD. This answer should be different for every single program, so make sure you review the program's website and ASHP listing thoroughly.

5. What have you heard about our program?
Be honest. Well, not brutally honest. Talk about any positive things you've heard, and it's best to skip the negatives. Show that you have done your research or that you have talked to residents and students at that site.

6. What are your short and long-term career goals?
Be specific. For example, in the next two years I want to complete a PGY1 (and/or PGY2), publish a research project, become board certified (know the qualifications for eligibility and specialties offered), complete a teaching certificate, become a preceptor, etc. Long term, I want to work in a primary care clinic, precept students and residents, and hold an adjunct faculty position with a college of pharmacy.

7. Besides completing a residency, what other steps do you think you will have to take to reach your career goals?
Win the lottery? (No, don't say that). If you were asked question #6, tie this answer back to those goals. If you haven't yet been asked about your goals, now you can tie them into your answer. If you're interested in a specialty, find someone in that area of practice to discuss your questions. Focus on board certification, teaching certificate, certificate programs through ASHP/APhA, attending specific conferences (ASHP's Preceptor Conference, IDWeek, ADA's Annual Meeting, etc.), or utilizing a mentorship program.

8. What areas of pharmacy practice are you most interested in?
Goldilocks theory: avoid saying you're open to everything but also don't come off as only wanting to do to one specific thing. I know, it sounds like walking a tightrope, but you can do it. Express that you have particular interests in 1-2 areas, but that you look forward to a well-rounded PGY1 program. With additional experiences, you may find that the areas of practice you found interesting as a student will change once you become a pharmacist.

9. What disease states are you most interested in?
See previous question and the Goldilocks theory.

10. What are three of your strengths?
No one should be surprised by this or the following question. My main advice would be to think of strengths that are unique to you. If everyone answers that they are dedicated, passionate, and hardwork-

ing, those adjectives lose all meaning. If you need assistance, try asking your friends, family, and preceptors about your strengths. You may also find preceptor-identified strengths already listed in previous APPE evaluations.

11. What are three of your areas for improvement (aka nice way to say weaknesses)?
While I would definitely give you bonus points for quoting The Office, please do not say "I work too hard, I care too much, and sometimes I can be too invested in my job." The trick to this one is, I'm looking for someone who can objectively identify their weaknesses *and* show actionable steps in improving. A classic weakness example is "public speaking," but that is only half the answer. The most important part of that answer would be to share that you have asked to do extra presentations on rotations and will continue to do so during residency to gain public speaking confidence. This cannot be stressed enough, but it's absolutely imperative to have areas of improvement that you can express ways to actually improve. Don't give an example of not being assertive enough then not explain ways that you have, can, or will improve that weakness. Give me an example of how you conquered this by having a critical conversation with a difficult patient or approaching a physician with an important clinical recommendation.

12. What three words would you use to describe yourself? Don't let the more relaxed version of this question throw you off. This is just another way to ask about your strengths and personality.

13. What role do you typically take in group projects?
Another Goldilocks question: don't say you always want to be in charge but don't tell me that you always just follow. Talk about wanting to lead when appropriate but are happy to play a supporting role if someone else is more qualified. If you're tasked to work with your RPD or the hospital CEO, you're probably not going to want to try to grab the leadership reigns. I want a resident who can read group dynamics, initiate and facilitate communication, and listen and adapt. It's best if you can give an example about how you previously worked in a successful group.

14. What has been your proudest achievement?
This is a chance to highlight something unique about yourself and your experiences that hasn't yet come up in conversion. Did you conquer Mount Everest? Were you published in a prestigious medical journal? Did you help a newly diagnosed heart failure patient understand his new medication regime and self-care recommendations? It can be professional or personal, on your CV or not.

15. Can you tell me about XXXX on your CV?
Be prepared to discuss anything on your CV, including work experience, presentations, research, rotations, or anything else you have freely provided. Just like social media, if you make the information public, consider asking about it as fair game. You will most likely be asked about a particular project that interests the preceptor or a unique experience that they aren't familiar with. This should give you confidence

to tell a story that only you know (no one else will be aware if you remembered all the details correctly).

16. What sets you apart from your peers?
Use this as your chance to drive home what is most important about you. If you cannot think of a unique answer, why would a program rank you highly on their list? Be creative, everyone says that they are passionate, put patient care first, or want to help people. If you must provide one of those answers, at least give a special example of how you walk the talk. I can still remember a PGY2 candidate divulging how she helped her cousin with proper inhaler so he wouldn't have to quit playing soccer and wanting to help others who don't have strong family support. Another memorable response was a PGY1 candidate who took a semester off of school to help family members in Puerto Rico after the devastation of Hurricane Maria.

17. What has been your favorite APPE rotation?
Pick a rotation relevant to the program and then provide specific supporting examples. You may have been able to assist a resident with a research project. You may have had a particular patient who really touched your heart. But always avoid saying how you liked a rotation because it was easy or because you got to do it virtually in your sweatpants.

18. What has been your least favorite APPE rotation?
This can be a tricky question to answer. You always want to avoid blaming others for a poor experience. Consider possible answers related to COVID-19 and altered rotation experiences. 1) My infectious disease

experience was during the pandemic. Unfortunately, I was unable to obtain any hands-on experience with patients, but it was exciting to review the emerging treatment options for COVID-19 and relate them back to patient care. 2) My ambulatory care APPE afforded me a lot of great patient care opportunities with diverse medical conditions. While I learned a lot about telehealth, I was unable to complete any in-person visits, which limited my autonomy.

19. What was your favorite course in pharmacy school?
Again, pick something relevant to your strengths or the individual program. If you loved compounding, talk about how compounding requires creativity, which you love because you enjoy finding new solutions to problems. If you enjoyed a research methods class, related that back to the opportunity to conduct a longitudinal research project as a resident. Be sure to explain how your answer relates to you interest in the specific program.

20. How do you stay organized?
Give concrete examples: lists, calendars, sticky notes, color coordinating, etc. It's also an opportunity to note that you expect residency to require multiple experiences and projects with varying deadlines, and how your personal organization techniques will translate well.

21. What do you do to manage stress?
Stress, weakness, and vulnerability are all things humans experience and are okay. ASHP is looking to focus on resident well-being and preventing burn-

out. You can once again show your personality with this question. Whether you enjoy spending time with your animals, lifting weights, reading, riding roller coasters, or playing basketball, it's great to show that you're a real person. I would, however, suggest ensuring your answers are appropriate for an interview setting. It's a fine balance between being informal and unprofessional. You can tell me about your love of painting while still professionally omitting the part where you require a full bottle of wine and no pants. Know how to read a room and follow the mood of your interviewers.

22. How do you handle criticism?

Throughout residency training, you're going to be provided with formal and informal feedback on every rotation, presentation, and project you complete. The best answer is that you actively seek out constructive criticism and use it to grow personally and professionally.

23. How do you handle change?

Even if you have a strong disdain for change, you need to express how easily you can adapt to changes in schedules and expectations. I tend to eat the same foods every day, watch the same tv shows over and over, and keep to my daily schedule like clockwork but that isn't how I would answer an interview question about unexpected changes. Giving a specific example of how you adapted to change is key. You can also reiterate your organizational strategies and how they assist you in pivoting from one task to another.

24. What do you enjoy outside of pharmacy?
For this one, they just want to get to know you. Talk about your family, pets, travel, sports, food, etc. Naturally, people tend to gravitate towards those with similar interests, but the point is talking about yourself and your interests humanizes the interview process. This question can also help ease nerves during the interview, so it may be asked earlier in the day to develop rapport.

25. What makes a good leader?
Thought provoking question. To me, I want a leader who wouldn't order me to do something that they wouldn't do themselves. This comes up in science fiction and military novels; great leaders are respected because their subordinates see them on the front lines doing everything they have ordered others to do. Also, a leader needs to listen to their team, be open to suggestions, and push for innovation and creativity in the workplace. This is ultimately a personal question that you should think about for yourself.

26. What experience do you have with research?
It doesn't matter how big or small the experience, talk it up to sound important. If you designed, completed, and published a randomized control trial…WOW. However, assisting in IRB submission, data collection, data analysis, and manuscript writing are all valuable experiences that will translate well into your required research project during residency. Assessing a candidate's experience with research typically weighs heavily into the decision to interview a candidate or not, so I highly recommended you at least dip a toe

into this area. If you have no experience, be prepared to talk about your potential research interests, use the question to ask about current resident research, and even discuss a recent clinical trial that you reviewed for a journal club.

27. How do you feel about precepting students?
Obviously, you need to be interested in this or at least open to it. As a resident you will more likely than not help to orient, precept, and evaluate students throughout the year. You can talk about special residents or preceptors you have had and why they were impactful on your career. You can also turn this question around and ask the program about the role their residents play in student precepting.

28. What is your teaching style?
First of all, your teaching style should adapt to the individual learner, not vice versa. Second, ASHP defines and requires four preceptor roles to use during residency training: direct instruction, modeling, coaching, and facilitating, with the goal of independence. Direct instruction involves assigned readings, discussions, and other means of sharing content. Modeling involves having a learner observe while also thinking out loud. Coaching occurs when the workload shifts to the learner but the preceptor is there to provide direct feedback and support when needed. Facilitation is similar to independence, however the preceptor is available for assistance and discussion when needed. Bringing up these preceptor roles will show that you're invested in both precepting and residency training.

29. How would you incorporate student learning into your daily work life?

    Some may candidates may look at potential student precepting as too time consuming but students are capable of expanding patient care through patient interviews, drug information, projects, and other tasks pharmacists cannot always find the time to complete during a regular work day. For example, in many ambulatory care clinics, patient volumes would have to be significantly lower without a constant stream of APPE students to facilitate their care.

30. What characteristics make a good preceptor?

    This may sound like an abstract question, but I'm looking for concrete examples. Think about your favorite APPE preceptor and discuss specific examples of why you thought they were amazing.

31. How would you feel about being trained by pharmacists who do not have a PharmD degree?

    You have to respect everyone; an experienced non-residency trained pharmacist has a lot of practical knowledge and experience that you cannot acquire without years of hard work. Aside from pharmacists, you will likely learn more than you could imagine from pharmacy technicians about sterile compounding, medication use systems, and how the pharmacy actually functions. There is something to be learned from everyone.

32. While counseling a patient, you realize you are late to a meeting, what do you do?

    This answer should show where your priorities are. I would certainly put patient care over anything else; I would rather get in trouble for being late to a meeting, than abandon a patient who needed me. That said, you also want to show you're respectful to those you're meeting. One suggestion would be to step out of the patient room for a moment to notify at least one person, who will also be attending the meeting, that you will be late due to patient care.

33. While staffing, you catch a medication error by one of you co-residents, what do you do?
Do you ignore it? Talk to your co-resident? Tell everyone about it? Report it to your RPD? I would first correct the issue if the resident isn't present (we still need to take care of the patient first), then speak with them privately. No one feels good about making an error, so tread lightly.

34. Describe the work environment in which you are most productive.
I'm looking for someone who works well under pressure, wants to be challenged, and can adapt to unpredictable changes. If this doesn't sound like you, please reconsider your post-graduate plans. Those three descriptions are common in a resident's day to day life.

35. When do you feel it is justified to go against a hospital policy or procedure?
This can be a difficult question to answer. Do you follow every rule unquestionably? Do you disregard the rules if you don't agree with something? I think it's important to know and follow hospital policies and procedures. They were developed in the inter-

est of patient care and standardization. I would talk about potential gray areas in the policies or emerging situations that aren't clearly defined. In those instances, you should do what is clinically justified and in the best interest of patient safety (while still following applicable pharmacy laws and regulations pertinent to your state of practice).

36. What are your plans if you do not match this cycle?
In this answer, I would stress that completing a residency is necessary to reach your personal and professional goals. For those reasons, you would work for the next year to challenge yourself to grow and gain additional experiences. Don't speak in generalities: before your interviews, create a list of specific and actionable goals should you not match. Examples include completing ASHP's medication safety and informatics certificate programs, an online Master of Public Health degree, becoming involved in your state pharmacy organizations, and attending a specific national conference.

37. What is the most important factor to you when deciding to rank a program?
This question does require some soul searching. Do you want to complete a PGY2? Do you want to be in a program that can regularly hire residents? Is there a certain specialty you're pursuing? Are you invested in a certain community? Would you prefer to be the only resident or part of a large cohort of co-residents? There are a number of other factors to consider. I would urge you to think about this prior to your applications and certainly before interviews.

38. What questions were you prepared to be asked that we did not ask you?
    This is one of my favorite questions during interviews. It provides the program with insight into your preparation and allows you to bring up a talking point that shows off your unique skills or experiences.

EXAMPLE QUESTIONS: BEHAVIORAL

Behavioral-type questions will all require specific examples and provide insight into whether or not you're all talk. The good thing here is that no one will know if your examples are one hundred percent truthful or not. I would strongly urge you to reflect on the last couple of years and make notes about specific examples for each question. Since these answers will all be very specific to your experiences, I can only provide you with brief tips below.

Tell me about a time you...

39. Dealt with an upset patient.
    I want to hear that you listened to the patient's concerns and how you remedied the situation.

40. Made a mistake and how you corrected it.
    Everyone makes mistakes, but do you resolve and own up to them?

41. Went above and beyond for a patient.
    I'm looking for something truly above and beyond, not part of a normal pharmacy student's experience.

42. Had to work with someone with whom you did not get along.
    Not everyone is going to be best friends. As an RPD, can I trust you to work with a wide variety of professionals?

43. Improved a process at work or on rotations.
    Everyone wants to surround themselves with individuals who can be innovative and creative.

44. Made a difficult decision.
    The decision isn't important but your process of analyzing a situation and how you acted is.

45. Made a recommendation that was not accepted.
    As pharmacists, we don't have full control of the patient care process. Subsequently, we're all faced with recommendations that are declined or ignored. How do you handle those rejections?

46. Had to make a quick decision.
    Again, the decision isn't important but tell me about your process of analyzing the situation and what you did as a result.

47. Tried and failed.
    Everyone fails from time to time, but I want to know if you're able to take failure as information and use it to improve yourself.

48. Were faced with conflict.
    The conflict itself isn't important but how did you resolve it. Were you argumentative? Ignored it? Talked it out?

49. Implemented a new process or workflow.
    Figuring out ways to be more productive and provide better care are attributes everyone in leadership positions are seeking. Even as a student, you can have huge impacts on processes and workflows. Oftentimes, those in the situation have been working them for months or years and are just used to it working that way. Coming in with a new set of eyes and perspective can open up the opportunities for preceptors and clinics to improve the way they work.

50. Impacted patient care.
    Be very specific, no vague, fluff answers.

51. Completed a long-term project and how you kept on track.
    Residency is going to be full of months-long and year-long projects, are you able to stay organized and on track?

EXAMPLE QUESTIONS: UNIQUE

The following questions are seemingly a bit random. Some programs will not ask any and others will choose several. Overall, the goal of these questions is to better see your personality. While there are no right or wrong answers, creativity is encouraged. Also, it's another excellent opportunity to use your answers to highlight your personal and professional strengths. Don't just give a one-word answer but provide reasons for your responses. Since these answers will need to be personal and creative, I'll use my answers as examples.

52. If you were a drug (variants: animal, candy bar, food, restaurant, etc.), what drug would you be?

    If I were a drug, I would be propranolol. I'm versatile and adapt well to a variety of situations, just like propranolol has a wide range of indications (akathisia, Afib, tremor, HTN, migraines, thyroid storm, and esophageal varices to name a few). [This answer helps highlight a personal strength and provides insight on my clinical knowledge.]

    As an ISTJ personality type, I feel I would be a wolf: I'm usually quiet and independent, but I also work well in groups, seek out new challenges, and am observant to details. [Don't pick the obvious answer of cat or dog, really think about your unique personality.]

53. You're stranded on a deserted island, what 3 items do you take?

    I'm nothing if not practical, so for survival purposes I'm choosing food rations, fire starter, and cooking pot. [Really, I want to say a phone or boat, but that defeats the purpose of the exercise.]

54. When the zombie apocalypse hits, which 3 people are you teaming up with?

    I place high value on teamwork and problem solving so I choose MacGyver, Elon Musk, and one of the MythBusters. With this group, I know we can safely navigate the post-apocalyptic world with terrifyingly clever inventions.

55. Everyone always asks for a fun fact, but can you tell me a boring fact about you?

I'm way too organized and prepare too much. For example, if I know I'll be having cereal for breakfast the next day, I'll set out a bowl, spoon, and cereal box the night before.
Bonus boring fact: Chewy Chips Ahoy cookies are way better than Oreos.

56. What profession would you pursue if not pharmacy?
My plan was to become a physical therapist; I enjoy physical activity and promoting health and wellness. Aside from not really wanting to be hands on with patients, I chose pharmacy because I knew it would allow me to continue learning for the entirety of my career.

57. What advice would you give yourself starting pharmacy school?
Don't put so much emphasis on letter grades. Learning and understanding are far more valuable than acing an exam.

58. What would you do if you won $1 million (or another amount)?
I'll give the boring, practical answer here because it's part of my personality. I would pay off my loans, buy a home, and give the rest to my parents. If forced to choose something else, give me a classic V8 muscle car and vintage Teenage Mutant Ninja Turtle toys.

59. What's the last book you read (non-pharmacy related)?
I'm definitely a Star Wars nerd. For less than $5 per book, I keep reading one after another. It's a good escape from the stresses of everyday life.

60. What would you change about pharmacy school?
I learned a lot in pharmacology and pharmacotherapy but it all really came together during IPPE and especially APPE rotations. I would love to include more practical, real world applications of pharmacy knowledge and explore other pharmacist career paths. [I've learned way more as a pharmacist than I ever did in school. Don't be fooled, even experienced pharmacists are continually learning.]

61. If you could save one thing from your home, what would it be?
Assuming my family and pets are safe, I'm going in for my lockbox of valuable documents (homeowner's insurance, social security card, etc.). [What can I say? The common theme is that I'm practical. Don't be afraid to share a more personal item or family heirloom, if that's in your nature.]

62. If you could travel anywhere, where would you go?
Without a doubt, I'm choosing to go to Boston. It's where I'm from, and I've been many times since moving away. It's classic Americana: the religion of sports, diverse food culture, rolling hills, and storied history make me feel at home. [Remember that you're not being judged for you answer, be it the bottom of the ocean, the moon, or wherever else you may choose; we really do just want to get to know you since we'll be spending a whole lot of time together in the coming year.]

AnecDose (not in a bad way), guest edition: During PGY1 interviews, the interview panel asked the applicants to discuss three fun facts about themselves. One candidate talked about how her family adopted a Chihuahua puppy from a shelter, only weeks later to learn it was a coyote when they took it to the vet. Needless to say, she was remembered by the entire interview panel.

THE MOST DREADED QUESTION

63. What questions do you have?
    This is by far the hardest question to answer, yet it's certain to be asked multiple times. Most interviewers will save the last five to ten minutes for candidate questions, so the awkward factor goes up exponentially if you don't have any queries ready to go. As a director, I know this question can be daunting, and the most common response is "you've been answering most of my questions as we've been talking." Unfortunately, that answer isn't going to fly. You need some specific questions at your disposal. Remember that the interview isn't one sided: you should be trying to determine if you're interested in the program just as much as they are determining interest in you. Do not leave at the end of the day and regret not having asked more questions to help determine if the program is a good fit for you. I would prepare a list of at least 10 questions for everyone you interview with, even if you have to repeat questions in separate interview sessions. It's also okay to refer to your written list as needed; we know the whole interview process is stressful. Don't shy away from taking notes. Feel free to jot down

both answers to your questions and how you're feeling about the program throughout the day.

Sample questions to ask the RPD and preceptors:

- What research topics are you hoping residents choose next year?
- How often are you able to hire residents after residency?
- How do you provide feedback to residents?
- How often will I be interacting with the RPD?
- How are you identifying and combating potential resident burnout? (this is a big topic for ASHP!)
- Can you talk about the potential for early commitment for your PGY2 programs?
- What do you perceive to be the greatest strengths of this residency program?
- What are the key skills needed to succeed in this residency program?
- How do you incorporate layered learning with preceptors, residents, and students?
- If accredited: when is your next ASHP survey? Were any areas for improvement identified at the last survey?
- If pre-candidate or candidate status: when is your initial ASHP survey planned? Do you have any concerns about accreditation? Have you or the hospital gone through surveys of other programs?
- Tell me about your background, what brought you to this program/hospital?
- How do you incorporate resident feedback into making changes to the program?
- For preceptors, ask about their rotation experience. What is the patient population? How do you integrate

a resident? Asking about a specific rotation or specialty is a good way to get preceptors talking for several minutes.

AnecDose: A PGY2 candidate asked me, "So, are there a lot of hot, single doctors at your hospital?"

CLINICAL CASE

Many programs require a clinical case to help evaluate your clinical knowledge base. For my programs, I would write out a complicated patient case with a list of laboratory and physical results, multiple diagnoses, and a medication list. In addition to your clinical knowledge, I'm looking for how you problem solve and prioritize. Make sure to identify results that are outside of the normal range, consider drug-drug interactions, and evaluate for renal dose adjustments. When I review patient cases, whether fictional or in practice, I list out the current disease states and match up the corresponding medication list. This is an easy way to organize and identify which disease states are under- or over-treated. If given the option to write a SOAP note for 2-3 disease states, pick ones you're most familiar with. If I give you the choice, I expect you to be knowledgeable in those areas; now isn't the time to choose the hardest topics to show off. Even if you cannot remember guideline recommendations or specific dosing regimens, show that you can systematically review a patient profile. Also, if you can't remember guideline-recommended treatments or targets, explain where you would find the answer. At a minimum, be familiar with the names of major clinical guidelines and which drug information sources are reputable. Some programs will allow use of electronic references and some will not. To be safe, ensure you have Epocrates, Lexicomp, and/or Clinical Pharmacology downloaded, so you don't have to rely on internet searches or Wikipedia for your answers. Remember, it's easier for me to teach clinical knowledge than organization and preparation. Some cases will be written and some will be verbal discussions. You may be evaluated on your clinical knowledge base, thought process, and communication skills.

LUNCH WITH CURRENT RESIDENTS

The first couple hours have gone by in a blur, time for a slight break. Expect a go on a tour of the facility and have lunch with the current residents. I would advise you to pass on the spaghetti option or the sushi that has been marked down on clearance. This is your opportunity to learn about the program from a resident point of view, but is absolutely part of the evaluation process. You may meet residents who think their program is the best in the world and other residents who may be struggling with the workload or trying to recover from an unfavorable meeting with a physician earlier that day. Use each personal perspective as a data point, keeping in mind things are usually not as great (or bad) as they are made out to be. This period will certainly be a bit more relaxed; you may know the residents from pharmacy school or APPE rotations, but continue to be professional. The main questions I would ask the current residents as RPD are: what questions did the candidates ask and how did they act during lunch? Prepare for meeting with residents the same as you would for the other interviews. Use the questions below to help guide your conversations.

Samples questions to ask current residents:

- What was the biggest reason you were interested in this program?
- What is a typical day/week like for you?
- What rotations or experiences have been the most rewarding that you would recommend I pursue?
- What elective rotations do you wish you had chosen?
- What has surprised you most during residency?
- What expectations did you have before residency that changed once you started?
- What changes to the program do you expect for next year?
- How often do you interact with the RPD?
- How often do you interact with your co-residents?
- How do preceptors give you feedback?
- Tell me about your research project. How did you choose the topic? Who would you recommend as a research preceptor?
- How is your job search going? Are you interviewing for PGY2?
- What is the program doing to help prevent and identify resident burnout?
- What area of town do you recommend living in?

AnecDose: A candidate spent lunch telling my residents about how interested they were in other residency programs, just because they knew each other from school. Remember: everything said to the residents will get back to the RPD.

PRESENTATION

With a full belly and some built up camaraderie with the current residents, the spotlight reignites and all the attention returns to you. Expect to give a formal slideshow presentation; it may be a 20-minute presentation on a topic of your choice, a journal club review, or a simple self-introduction. If given the opportunity to choose your own topic, consider that there may be as many as 20 or more other candidates. Pick a topic that is both unique and relevant to the program's specialty or your interests. You don't want to show up for interviews and present on the same topic as another candidate. Also, it's far better to go really in depth on a specific subsection of a topic than trying to present everything about diabetes in 20 minutes. Assume the other residency candidates, current residents, preceptors, and RPD to be in attendance. We'll be taking fastidious notes as you talk, but try not to read into whether our transcriptions are positive or negative. Presentations are evaluated for content and your presentation skills; most pharmacy schools have standard evaluation rubrics for when you're on APPE rotations that you can refer to when creating and practicing your presentation.

When designing and delivering traditional slideshow presentations, be sure to:

- Write an attention-grabbing title (everyone enjoys a good pharmacy pun)
- Present objectives with action verbs (don't repeat the same verb twice)
    o Examples: apply, arrange, assess, calculate, classify, compare, construct, contrast, create, critique, define, demonstrate, describe, differentiate, discuss, distinguish, evaluate, examine,

explain, generate, identify, illustrate, interpret, list, modify, outline, predict, prepare, present, review, solve, summarize, and understand (29)
- Document references for all information presented that is not your own
    - I strongly suggest corresponding references on the bottom of each slide
- Utilize primary literature and evidence-based guidelines
- Conclude with a summary slide
- Adhere to allotted time limit
    - You will likely be "graded" down if you go over the time limit, especially if it's by a significant amount of time. Worst case scenario, you may even be asked to stop once you reach the maximum time limit.
- Limit use of notes, present in a conversational tone
- Provide slide handouts; if you have an important graph or algorithm, print this out full page
- Maintain eye contact with the audience
- Use appropriate speaking volume and rate
- Practice pronouncing difficult words (ie levetiracetam or ustekinumab)
- Avoid putting full sentences on your slides; slides should act as an outline of the information you will present verbally
- Be engaging! Incorporate audience participation and questions
- Repeat back questions asked by the audience; if you can't answer a question, say that you will get back to them (and don't forget to)

You have been giving formal presentations throughout pharmacy school and on APPE rotations, but you will likely still have some nervous energy. Keep in mind that you will probably have a better understanding of the topic than the audience. Even presenting to experienced pharmacists, they typically haven't researched and studied the material like you have in the week leading up to your interview. Additionally, I always go into presentation assuming that the audience is only listening to about half of what I say. Especially with other interview candidates, they're too nervous about their own presentations to pay you their full attention. Knowing they aren't hanging on my every word helps me relax.

> *AnecDose, guest edition: We had a candidate give a presentation that was fully plagiarized. You may think you can be slick when interviewing at a site far from where your school and rotations are, but pharmacy is a small world and inevitably someone will find out. You can certainly reuse (and update) one of you own presentations, but do not use or copy work that is not yours.*

CHECK OUT

You've made it to the finish line. Just one last step before you're free to loosen your tie, kick off your shoes, and breathe. This sounds like it's building up to one final terror... but it isn't. Checking out with the RPD is merely one final chance to address any questions you still have and exchange pleasantries. While I will never give you any indication, overtly or covertly, on where you stack up against the other candidates, I will want to express gratitude and point out something about you that impressed me. As the director of a program, I do want as many candidates as possible to rank us. After a long day, I don't expect any groundbreaking questions to conclude your interview. Simply make sure to express thanks. It also wouldn't hurt to mention anything you learned about the program that particularly interested you e.g. research opportunities, elective rotations, precepting students, collaborating with residents and preceptors from another site, or academic responsibilities. I think most RPDs would be flattered by compliments related to their personal research or the design of the residency program.

> *AnecDose, guest edition: One candidate left behind a small electronic device after her interview. When she came back later that day to collect it, she told us it was a USB drive. Unbeknownst to her, we had already researched it and discovered it was a recording device. She definitely left an impression on her interviewers because you absolutely cannot record interviews.*

POST-INTERVIEW

After each successive interview, your level of confidence will undoubtedly grow. Preparation and practice are great, but replicating the full interview experience can be challenging. Immediately after each interview, make notes for yourself: what positive impressions did the program give you? What negative thoughts did you have? Did you feel comfortable? Did the current residents seem to be enjoying their residency year? What questions do you wish you asked? What did you personally do well? What do you think you need to work on for the next interview? Did you get asked any challenging questions? Don't beat yourself down if you think you could have presented yourself better. Focus on what you did well and what actionable steps you can take to improve for next time. Your interview skills will be tested and you will see growth throughout the entirety of your working life.

Next, write your follow up thank you notes as soon as possible. Hand written cards and email are both acceptable forms of communication. I always enjoy a thoughtful, hand written note, but if the rank order deadline is quickly approaching or your interview was entirely remote, stick to email. For hand written notes, send them at least to the RPD. But if you want to send them to everyone who interviewed you, email might be easier. As an RPD, I'm not looking for another letter-of-intent-length note. A simple thank you and mentioning a particular part of the program that interests you is sufficient. I will definitely keep track of who sends a follow-up thank you and who doesn't.

Example:

> Dr. *<Name>*,
>
> Thank you for the opportunity to interview for and learn more about your residency program. I was excited to learn that you are expanding ambulatory care services to assist in transitions of care and medication safety. I hope that my experience with a Meds to Beds service can be valuable to you and your organization.
>
> Sincerely,
> *<Name>*

AnecDose: I once received a written thank you card that was so hastily written, I couldn't even read half of the words. Reading bad handwriting might be pharmacists' specialty, but it's better to be thoughtful and deliberate.

RANK ORDER LISTS

The matching process may seem complicated and top secret, but for you it should be quite simple. Don't try to guess how programs will rank you. Use the matching site to enter all the programs you liked, ordering them by your preference. While the PGY1 match rate was 63% in 2020, keep in mind that in Phase 1 specifically, 37% of applicants matched with their top choice, 13% matched with their second choice, 6% matched with their third choice, 3% matched with their fourth choice, 3% matched with their fifth or lower choice, and 38% went unmatched (3). While the average applicant ranked 4.3 programs, matched candidates ranked on average 5 programs while unmatched applicants ranked only 3 programs. It may seem obvious, but the more programs you rank, the better your chances of getting into one program or another. Listing only 1-2 programs will not increase your odds of matching with them. If you have been filling in your spreadsheet (Appendix 1) with pros and cons of each program as you interviewed, it can help you make your decision a bit more easily; however, don't entirely discount your gut feeling. Regardless of how you come to your ranking decisions, be sure to only rank the programs you're willing to go to. If you're going to rank 20 programs, you need to be mentally ready and okay if you match with #20. If you want to be picky, another important consideration is this:

would I rather match with Program X or have to go through Phase 2 of the Match?

> *AnecDose: One of my APPE students interviewed with 6 programs but was dead set on her top choice. She felt as though interviews went really well and decided to only rank that single program. She figured she had a pretty good chance at it, but otherwise she would do something else instead of residency. Jumping ahead to the release of the Match results, she found she did not match. This left her struggling to research and apply to other programs, but again, she unfortunately did not match in either Phase 2 or the scramble. She was a strong student with great experiences, so heed this example and the advice against being too picky.*

As an RPD or preceptor, I'm exhausted after interviews. I may have interviewed dozens of candidates, all having strengths and weaknesses. When deciding on a rank order list, we bring together everyone involved in interviews, including current residents. We go back and review everything from applications through interviews. Since these interviews have taken place over several weeks, it isn't possible to remember every detail of every candidate. Now I have to get a number of other pharmacists, perhaps even my boss, to come to a consensus on who to rank and how to rank them. Just like you, I don't want any of our positions to go unfilled and enter into Phase 2. Candidates may grade out very similarly, with some scoring better in different sections: application materials, letters of recommendation, interviews, or presentations. First, I need to determine if there are any candidates that I would definitely not want as a resident. As in, I would rather have an unfilled residency position than hire that candidate. Next, we need to agree on how to rank each candidate we liked. This process can become quite heated, and the rank order may mutate several times over one meeting. It's kind of like a puzzle where you start with the outside pieces and work way your way in; a couple candidates may be the obvious top choices, while others may be acceptable options but have scored lower across the board. It can be very challenging for us ranking current rotation students, especially if they will be ranked low or not at all. We know that our decisions will have an impact on a number of lives and careers. These are decisions we always take very seriously. There are often a lot of conflicting considerations. Aside from the objective measures from applications, interviews, clinical cases, and presentations, I usually have an overarching feeling about each candidate. Do we have months of experience with a candidate on rotation? Did someone complete a relevant research project? Do I remember someone's personal story and investment in pharmacy? Or did someone have a professionalism issue on rotations? Did someone fade into the crowd? Was an interview presentation poorly researched?

Unfortunately, there isn't one perfect equation to matching. Each program and candidate will have specific goals and needs. Use the insights, tips, and tricks you just read to avoid interview faux pas, maximize your objective scores, and learn how to positively **be memorable**.

VIRTUAL INTERVIEWS

March 2020: when daily life in the United States changed forever. Facing a pandemic that stunted travel and commerce, implemented "social distancing", and everyone masking up and bathing in hand sanitizer, video conferencing emerged as part of the new normal. The availability of Cisco Webex, Google Meet, Microsoft Teams, Skype, and Zoom have transformed the way we communicate. While many pharmacists were entrenched on the front lines (and protecting hydroxychloroquine and azithromycin supplies), telecommuting, virtual doctor's appointments, and remote APPE rotations became widespread. For prospective pharmacy residents and residency graduates alike, the job market's shift towards virtual interviews has been unprecedented. Similarly, the seasonal pharmacy-related conference schedule was forced to adapt, including ASHP's Midyear going virtual in 2020.

As with most changes in life, it's those who embrace challenges head on that are usually most successful. If you have never read Spencer Johnson's "Who Moved My Cheese" on dealing with change, I give you permission to pause reading this book and buy it now. While many of the basic recommendations for successful interviews hold true, the virtual environment does offer unique challenges. Below are my critical factors for virtual interviews.

1. Check your technology
   Strong Wifi connection is key. Make sure you know what platform will be used so you can test the system a day or so ahead of time and log in early, if possible, on interview day. Whether it's Teams, Zoom, Skype, Google, or any of the other myriad of options, you will feel more confident if you don't have to learn a brand-new program during your interview.

2. Avoid virtual backgrounds
   Sure, it's fun to chat with your friends with a fake sunny beach or the Golden Gate Bridge background.

Interviews are just not the time or place. At best, it will be distracting, and at worst it may be interpreted as unprofessional.

3. Remember your body language
   It's natural to act more casually at home compared to an onsite interview. But try to imagine you're sitting at a formal dinner table: sit upright and avoid putting your elbows on the desk or resting your chin on your hands. I've been guilty of this myself but try to focus on not rocking or spinning in your chair. One advantage is that you will be able to see yourself on the screen, so you can watch for proper body language.

4. Settle in a quiet place
   Find an area where you can hear yourself think and that has minimal background noise. Remind your family or roommate not to interrupt, secure your pets in another room, lock the door, and put your phone on silent. I prefer to use earbuds to cut down on background noise and prevent myself from leaning forward to speak into the computer microphone.

5. Dress for success
   We have all seen the commercials where meeting attendees dress professionally from the waist up and then, unfortunately, stand up to reveal pajama pants (or worse). Even though they can't see your whole outfit, consider dressing up fully. Dressing professionally from head to toe can act to improve your overall demeanor: it's easier to remember to act professionally if you're not lounging in yoga pants and flip flops.

6. Maintain eye contact
   Maintaining good eye contact is paramount during interviews and being physically separated but connected via a computer does not minimize the importance. The biggest problem is that you may actually be looking the other person directly in the eyes but the location on your screen may give them the perspective that you're looking in another direction. This forces us to maintain eye contact with our own webcam. My solutions to this problem are twofold: 1) align the video conference window so that the interviewer is close to your webcam and 2) place a photo of a friend, family member, or even pet proximal to your camera. This will act to improve eye contact and help you to relax.

7. Present smartly
   Virtual interviews offer you a tremendous reprieve during formal presentations. The single most stressful component of an interview may be standing up in front of a group of pharmacists and other residency candidates. With the remote option, you don't have to worry about how many people will be in the audience, whether or not you will have a podium, or where the closest bathroom is. However, there are still a few unique challenges. Make sure the information on your slides is clear and readable for someone viewing them online. Don't shuffle notes or papers in front of your computer's microphone (use electronic notes if needed). Before your interviews, close all unused programs and browser pages; you might not want us to accidently see all your private windows if you happen to share your screen. Utilize technology

to your advantage: incorporate engaging visuals and audience polls.

8. Don't be infamous
When you have a short break or you won't be speaking imminently, mute your microphone. For longer break periods that you will be away from your computer, remember to turn off your camera. You can also cover your webcam with a sticky note during breaks to be sure. Although, I'm always looking for an additional *AnecDoses* if your mic picks up your candid thoughts or you stand up to reveal your choice of unicorn PJs to compliment your suit jacket and tie.

AnecDose: During a virtual interview, the candidate had a laptop on an unstable tray. He was nervously shaking his leg making the entire screen bounce up and down for the entire time.

Bonus AnecDose: Many video conferencing programs allow you to enter your preferred name or nickname. One candidate must have forgotten that they had created a personal account previously with a username they wouldn't want repeated in front of their mama...don't do that. Double check that your account settings are appropriate for an interview.

CLOSING

ADVICE FROM OTHERS

I asked colleagues, friends, and former students the most important advice they would share with residency applicants, here's what they had to say:

Beth C.
PGY2 Ambulatory Care Residency Program Director

- A follow-up thank you is a nice gesture to send to the RPD and other interviewers. If you're close to the rank order deadline, an email is encouraged; however, if you choose to send a card, I would recommend having the card and pre-stamped envelope with you so you can write the thank you note and mail it out the same day as your interview.
- If you're applying to a PGY2, I would strongly recommend seeing if your PGY1 RPD can tailor your residency to include experiences (whether learning experiences, electives, presentations, research, etc.) in the field you're choosing to pursue. These will be great talking points at interviews to show your enthusiasm for the field and ability to take actionable steps towards reaching your career goals.
- I would highly encourage anyone to look for residencies outside of their location comfort zone. It can

be challenging to pack up and relocate, but keep in mind it's just one year, and if the residency experiences connect better with your goals, it will definitely be worth it in the long run.

Michael L.
Former PGY1 Pharmacy Practice Residency Program Director and PGY2 Critical Care Residency Program Director

- Remember that interviews go both ways. You should be trying to determine if you're really interested in each program. Rely on the experiences of current residents, they will tell you the details that program directors may not even be aware of.
- I don't look for the best or smartest candidates, I look for the best candidate for our specific program.

John R.
PGY1 Pharmacy Practice Residency Program Director

- I can easily teach clinical knowledge and even communication skills and confidence. What I can't teach is how to have compassion for patients, dedication to hard work, and respect for cultural diversity.
- At residency showcase events, I want the candidates to focus on speaking with my current residents. When you do talk to a program director, don't ask questions that are clearly outlined on the website. I remember at least ten negative interactions for every one positive.

Michelle V.
PGY2 Ambulatory Care Resident

- Make sure to gather your letters of recommendation early to ensure they are submitted before the deadline. Keep track of who hasn't submitted theirs and stay on top of them to make sure it's in on time (preceptors and faculty are busy, especially right before winter break, and may not meet the deadline if you ask too late). I'd also recommend having a backup letter of recommendation, if possible, just in case.
- Familiarize yourself with everything on your CV because anything is fair game and many of your experiences may be from 2-3 years prior.
- Be open minded for all of you interviews, you'll get a good feel for your potential daily work environment and preceptors that may change your preferences. For both PGY1 and PGY2, my final rank list order turned out differently than what I originally expected.
- Once you start residency, be open to new opportunities and changes. You may feel like you don't know what you're doing being a recent grad and that's ok. Preceptors are there to teach and guide you through the process, and you really do know more than you think. Your knowledge, confidence, and independence will grow over time, so make the best of every opportunity.

Megan D.
PGY2 Pediatric Resident

- Be proactive. Some programs get over 100 applications every year and only interview 20-25 candidates. Do a research project, present at Midyear or another

pharmacy conference, intern or volunteer at a hospital, run for a leadership position, and publish something. Anything! There are numerous student publications, even if it's just in a hospital newsletter, that counts too.
- Choose clinical and competitive APPE rotations that require an application. This will allow you to gain valuable experience, help determine your career interests, and potentially spend several months with residency preceptors and leadership.

Casey J.
PGY1 Pharmacy Practice Resident

- Interviews are stressful for everyone. I would go into each one with the goal of learning as much about the program as you can. If you focus on how nervous you are or how stressful the day is, that will show off in all your interactions. What's the worst thing that happens, they don't like you? Just move on to the next one.
- One of my main career goals is to be in academia so I focused on programs affiliated with a college of pharmacy. I wanted to gain as much experience giving lectures and working in skills lab with students so those aspects were important when searching for programs. Figure out what you really want and then look for programs that can help you reach your goals.

Baxter S.
PGY1 Pharmacy Practice Resident

- I would encourage students to be open to moving to a new city, if only for a year. Since I was looking

to move cross country, I also targeted programs with multiple residents to have a built-in support system. Try to think about what daily life would be for you as a resident and compare the different benefits programs offer. If you like 2 programs pretty evenly but one has twice the vacation time, that's a no brainer for me.
- Don't overthink it when you submit your rank order list. Don't try to guess which programs will rank you the highest. Honestly, just put them in the order of your interest and be done with it. Also, remember if you rank a program last on your list you should be ready to go there. One of my classmates ranked every program he interviewed with and ended up matching somewhere he didn't really want to be.

Jennifer P.
NICU Clinical Pharmacy Specialist (previous PGY2 Pediatric Resident)

- It's never too early to start preparing your application materials. Once APPE rotations start, each month will pass by in a whirlwind; use any available time to start writing letters of intent, update your CV, and research potential residency programs.
- Ask for four letters of recommendation if three are required, there's always a small chance one doesn't get submitted on time, especially when programs have earlier deadlines.

Matt M.

Emergency Department Clinical Pharmacist (previous PGY1 Pharmacy Resident)

- Your CV and letters of intent are vital to making a good first impression, have them reviewed by someone who will give you honest and objective advice.
- Remember professionalism always. Even if you know the current residents, it doesn't mean you can act unprofessionally or think you get special treatment whether on rotations or at the Midyear showcase.
- When choosing a program, for me it was all about the "family feel". How is the support system? What's the relationship between the current residents, pharmacy staff, and leadership? You will spend the majority of you waking life during residency at work so make sure you feel wanted and comfortable in the program or you will likely burn out.

FINAL REMARKS

Now in my tenth year as a practicing pharmacist (writing this book, I feel like I was just in your shoes yesterday), I can confidently say that finding happiness in your profession while never putting your family life second is of the utmost importance. If you get burned out five or ten years into your career or come home to an unhappy environment, what then? Several studies reveal that over fifty percent of practicing pharmacists are burnt out, experiencing emotional exhaustion, depersonalization, and a reduced sense of personal achievement (30-33). Find your passion, whether ambulatory care, management, pediatrics, critical care, or any other specialty, and never let fear hold you back. Whether you're just starting year one of pharmacy school, actively preparing residency application materials, or a licensed, working pharmacist, you can improve the strength of your application and interview skills today. Imagine a car company that puts tremendous research and development resources into creating a carbon-neutral, sleek, and durable vehicle that remains unsold at the dealership because there's no marketing plan or sales pitch. After all the years you have or will have dedicated academically, don't let yourself sit rusting on the lot. I urge you to put in at least as much time and effort into obtaining your desired residency as you would in preparing for the NAPLEX or MPJE exams. Don't be afraid to seek out residency training and don't hesitate to reapply if you didn't match previously. While I keep bringing up the 63% PGY1 match rate in 2020, remember there were 3,924 positions available, so heed the advice in these pages and get *MATCHED*.

If you need personal assistance, please visit www.apothecademy.com or contact me directly at bleonard@apothecademy.com. The following services are provided one on one or as group workshops:

- CV and letter of intent review
- Mock interviews
- Formal presentation review and practice sessions
- Mock case studies
- Residency portfolio review and scoring
- Professional mentoring
- Coming soon: NAPLEX and MPJE review

BIBLIOGRAPHY

1. *ASHP 2021 Match Statistics Match Trends.* (2020). National Matching Services Inc. https://natmatch.com/ashprmp/stats.html.
2. ASHP. (2020). *Summary Results of the Match for Positions Beginning in 2020 Combined Phase I and Phase II Residencies and Programs.* National Matching Services Inc. https://natmatch.com/ashprmp/stats/2020progstats.pdf.
3. ASHP. (2020). *Summary Results of the Match for Positions Beginning in 2020 Combined Phase I and Phase II Applicants.* National Matching Services Inc. https://natmatch.com/ashprmp/stats/2020applstats.pdf.
4. ACCP. (2019). *Number of Pharmacy Degrees Conferred 1965–2019.* https://www.aacp.org/sites/default/files/2020-05/fall-2019-pps-degrees-conferred.pdf.
5. ASHP. (2020, March). *Guidance Document for the ASHP Accreditation Standard for Postgraduate Year One (PGY1) Pharmacy Residency Programs.* https://www.ashp.org/-/media/assets/professional-development/residencies/docs/guidance-document-PGY1-standards.ashx-?la=en&hash=20D275DC632B78E92626D7233DF52747279FE820.
6. ASHP. (2017, March). *PGY1 Pharmacy Residency Exemption Process.* https://www.ashp.org/-/media/assets/professional-development/residencies/docs/pgy1-residency-exemption-criteria.ashx.

7. ASHP. (2018). *ASHP Online Residency Directory.* https://accreditation.ashp.org/directory/#/program/residency.
8. ASHP. (2019, September). *ASHP Regulations on Accreditation of Pharmacy Residencies.* https://www.ashp.org/-/media/assets/professional-development/residencies/docs/accreditation-regulations-residencies.ashx?la=en&hash=266670210632AD9E4B2C31BF-F1A7D8D8FE8893DF.
9. *Occupational Outlook Handbook: Pharmacists.* (2020, September 1). U.S. Bureau of Labor Statistics. https://www.bls.gov/ooh/healthcare/pharmacists.htm.
10. *Pharmacy Demand Report (PDR) Executive Summary.* (2020). Pharmacy Workforce Center, Inc. https://www.aacp.org/sites/default/files/2020-10/pharmacy-demand-report-10062020.pdf.
11. Rodriguez de Bittner, M., Adams, A. J., Burns, A. L., Ha, C., Hilaire, M. L., Letendre, D. E., Scheckelhoff, D. J., Schwinghammer, T. L., Traynor, A., Zgarrick, D. P., & Bradley-Baker, L. R. (2011). Report of the 2010-2011 Professional Affairs Committee: Effective Partnerships to Implement Pharmacists' Services in Team-Based, Patient-Centered Healthcare. *American Journal of Pharmaceutical Education,* 75(10), S11. https://doi.org/10.5688/ajpe7510s11.
12. PHORCAS2020. (2020). ASHP PhORCAS. https://portal.phorcas.org/.
13. National Matching Services Inc. (2020). *ASHP Resident Matching Program.* https://natmatch.com/ashprmp/.
14. National Matching Services Inc. (2020). *The 2021 ASHP Match Schedule of Dates.* https://natmatch.com/ashprmp/schedule.html.
15. U.S. News & World Report L.P. (2020). *Best Pharmacy Schools.* https://www.usnews.com/best-graduate-schools/top-health-schools/pharmacy-rankings.

16. ASHP. (2020). Number of Applicants Applying for PGY1 Programs by School, 2020 Match- Combined Phase I and Phase II. National Matching Services Inc. https://natmatch.com/ashprmp/stats/2020schlstats-pgy1.pdf.
17. APhA. (2020). *Certificate Training Programs.* https://www.pharmacist.com/certificate-training-programs.
18. ASHP. (2020). *Professional Certificates-ASHP.* ASHP Professional Development. https://www.ashp.org/Professional-Development/Professional-Certificate-Programs.
19. ASHP. (n.d.). *PhORCAS Recommendation Form.* Retrieved October 10, 2020, from https://www.ashp.org/-/media/assets/professional-development/residencies/docs/phorcas-recommendation-form.ashx.
20. ASHP. (2020). *Midyear Clinical Meeting 2020 - ASHP.* https://midyear.ashp.org/.
21. ASHP. (2020). *PPS Candidates - ASHP Midyear Clinical Meeting.* https://midyear.ashp.org/PPS/PPS-Candidates?loginreturnUrl=SSOCheckOnly.
22. Hardouin, S., Cheng, T. W., Mitchell, E. L., Raulli, S. J., Jones, D. W., Siracuse, J. J., & Farber, A. (2020). RETRACTED: Prevalence of unprofessional social media content among young vascular surgeons. *Journal of Vascular Surgery,* 72(2), 667–671. https://doi.org/10.1016/j.jvs.2019.10.069.
23. Cain, J., Scott, D. R., & Smith, K. (2010). Use of social media by residency program directors for resident selection. *American Journal of Health-System Pharmacy,* 67(19), 1635–1639. https://doi.org/10.2146/ajhp090658.
24. Go, P. H., Klaassen, Z., & Chamberlain, R. S. (2012). Residency selection: do the perceptions of US programme directors and applicants match? *Medical Education,* 46(5), 491–500. https://doi.org/10.1111/j.1365-2923.2012.04257.x.

MATCHED | 93

25. Go, P. H., Klaassen, Z., & Chamberlain, R. S. (2012). Attitudes and Practices of Surgery Residency Program Directors Toward the Use of Social Networking Profiles to Select Residency Candidates: A Nationwide Survey Analysis. *Journal of Surgical Education*, 69(3), 292–300. https://doi.org/10.1016/j.jsurg.2011.11.008.
26. Buckley, K., Karr, S., Nisly, S. A., & Kelley, K. (2018). Evaluation of a mock interview session on residency interview skills. *Currents in Pharmacy Teaching and Learning*, 10(4), 511–516. https://doi.org/10.1016/j.cptl.2017.12.021.
27. Caballero, J., Benavides, S., Steinberg, J. G., Clauson, K. A., Gauthier, T., Borja-Hart, N. L., & Marino, J. (2012). Development of a residency interviewing preparatory seminar. *American Journal of Health-System Pharmacy*, 69(5), 400–404. https://doi.org/10.2146/ajhp110345.
28. Koenigsfeld, C. F., Wall, G. C., Miesner, A. R., Schmidt, G., Haack, S. L., Eastman, D. K., Grady, S., & Fornoff, A. (2012). A Faculty-Led Mock Residency Interview Exercise for Fourth-Year Doctor of Pharmacy Students. *Journal of Pharmacy Practice*, 25(1), 101–107. https://doi.org/10.1177/0897190011431632.
29. Bloom, B. S. (1956). *Taxonomy of Educational Objectives, Handbook 1: Cognitive Domain* (2nd edition Edition). Addison-Wesley Longman Ltd.
30. Ball, A. M., Schultheis, J., Lee, H.-J., & Bush, P. W. (2020). Evidence of burnout in critical care pharmacists. *American Journal of Health-System Pharmacy*, 77(10), 790–796. https://doi.org/10.1093/ajhp/zxaa043.
31. Durham, M. E., Bush, P. W., & Ball, A. M. (2018). Evidence of burnout in health-system pharmacists. *American Journal of Health-System Pharmacy*, 75(23_Supplement_4), S93–S100. https://doi.org/10.2146/ajhp170818.

32. Kang, K., Absher, R., & Granko, R. P. (2020). Evaluation of burnout among hospital and health-system pharmacists in North Carolina. *American Journal of Health-System Pharmacy*, 77(6), 441–448. https://doi.org/10.1093/ajhp/zxz339.

33. Kraus, S., Gardner, N., Jarosi, N., McMath, T., Gupta, A., & Mehta, B. (2020). Assessment of burnout within a health-system pharmacy department. *American Journal of Health-System Pharmacy*, 77(10), 781–789. https://doi.org/10.1093/ajhp/zxaa042.

APPENDIX

Appendix 1: Sample Residency Program Comparison Chart

Characteristics	Program 1	Program 2
Location		
Hospital size		
RPD		
Application deadline		
Accreditation status		
Salary		
Average number of hours worked per week		
Weekend requirements		
Number of days off		
Number of holidays off and required to work		
Parking costs		
Office space		
Other benefits		
Number of residents		
Required rotations		
Elective rotations		
PGY2 programs at site		

Paid conference attendance		
Paid professional membership		
Research and project requirements		
Presentation requirements		
Teaching certificate program		
Post-Midyear notes		
Post-interview notes		
Notes from current residents		
Current positions of previous residents		
Notes from classmates on rotation at site or who also interviewed		

Appendix 2: Sample Residency Candidate Self-Evaluation

Review this abbreviated application evaluation tool. Example experiences for each category are listed by tier levels, with Tier 1 being the lowest and Tier 5 being the highest. Use this guide to help build your residency portfolio by adding experiences in higher tier levels. For a more detailed review with actionable goal setting, visit www.apothecademy.com.

	Tier 1	Tier 2	Tier 3	Tier 4	Tier 5
Pharmacy school rank	>100	Top 100	Top 50	Top 25	Top 10
GPA	3.0-3.19	3.2-3.39	3.4-3.59	3.6-3.79	3.8-4.0
Other degrees (excluding PharmD and Bachelor's)			Master's or PhD not related to pharmacy		MBA, MPA, Master of Education, or similar
Work experience: type	Non-pharmacy	Non-pharmacy management	Research	Retail, MTM	Hospital
Work experience: length	<1 year	1-2 years	2-3 years	3-5 years	>5 years
Awards and honors	Scholarships	Employee recognition	State and pharmacy school awards	Honor society	National awards
Leadership	Local chair	Local treasurer or secretary	Event organizer; pharmacy advocacy	Local president or VP; other national position	National-level president or VP
Research	Laboratory assistant	Assisting with non-pharmacy research	Assisting with pharmacy research	Authoring a non-pharmacy research project	Authoring a pharmacy research project

Posters and publications	Newsletter publication	One poster presentation	Multiple poster presentations	Non-clinical publication	Clinical publication
Number of patient care APPE rotations	0-2		3-5		6 or more
Certificates	BLS and immunization only		1-2 additional certificates		3 or more additional certificates
Service	0-3 volunteer projects	4-5 volunteer projects	6 or volunteer projects	Medical missions' trip	Organization of community outreach

ABOUT THE AUTHOR

First time on my own, my path to becoming a pharmacist unknowingly began in the middle of nowhere (DeLand, FL) on the campus of Stetson University. There were a limitless number of possible career paths. It was shortly after the dot-com bubble burst of the early 2000's but it was evident that computer programming would present cutting edge job opportunities and career growth. It was there, during college orientation, that I decided to major in computer science and help shape the technological future. Fast forward mere days later, I turned to my roommate and declared "I'm changing my major!" The first day of class, first homework assignment, and I had no idea what I was doing. In a matter of days, my fool-proof plan had been thwarted by my ineptitude to master the first assignment of computer science 101. For the next year I carried on taking a variety of classes as an undecided, before focusing on courses I enjoyed and majoring in integrative health sciences. Physics, chemistry, biology, nutrition, anatomy, and physiology were far more up my alley than trying to code my way onto the computer science track, but I still had not even thought about becoming a pharmacist. With my interests in exercise, health, and wellness, I was planning on becoming a physical therapist through my sophomore and junior years. Ultimately, the hands-on nature of physical therapy and rehabilitation was a major downside for this introvert. As much as anyone hates to admit it, mom and dad are usually right. My mom had simply asked, "Why not become a pharmacist? That involves math and science." The eureka moment. After scrambling to take the Pharmacy College Admission Test (PCAT) and submit applications, pharmacy became my new career goal, albeit with little to no exposure to the field.

I realized ambulatory care as my passion during my eight-week APPE rotation with a primary care pharmacist at UF. She not only had the clinical freedom to manage diabetes, hypertension, and anticoagulation, but also established meaningful and long-lasting relationships with patients. After receiving my Doctor of Pharmacy (PharmD) degree in 2011, I completed an ambulatory care focused PGY1 residency in 2012. Over the course of my career, I have worked in emergency medicine, long-term care, hospital-based outpatient clinics, primary care, and population health. Through all of this, I found the most fulfilling aspects of being a pharmacist have been time spent mentoring students and creating a PGY2 Ambulatory Care Pharmacy Residency Program. As a residency preceptor, coordinator, and director, I have been heavily involved in both PGY1 and PGY2 candidate application review, recruitment, onsite interviews, and final candidate rankings for multiple programs. In addition to being a licensed pharmacist in Tennessee and Florida, I hold a consultant pharmacist license in Florida and national board certification in ambulatory care and geriatrics. My experience also includes pharmacy student career coach at the University of Florida, APPE rotation preceptor, NAPLEX question bank reviewer for Kaplan Test Prep, and continuing education field tester for the American Pharmacists Association (APhA) and American Society of Health-System Pharmacists (ASHP).

Made in the USA
Las Vegas, NV
05 November 2023

80292016R00066